THE SOHO BIBLIOGRAPHIES
XVI
RONALD FIRBANK

A BIBLIOGRAPHY OF
RONALD FIRBANK
SECOND EDITION

BY

MIRIAM J. BENKOVITZ

CLARENDON PRESS · OXFORD
1982

Oxford University Press, Walton Street, Oxford OX2 6DP
London Glasgow New York Toronto
Delhi Bombay Calcutta Madras Karachi
Kuala Lumpur Singapore Hong Kong Tokyo
Nairobi Dar es Salaam Cape Town
Melbourne Auckland
and associate companies in
Beirut Berlin Ibadan Mexico City

Published in the United States by
Oxford University Press, New York

© Miriam Benkovitz 1963, 1982

First edition published by Rupert Hart-Davis 1963
Second edition published by Oxford University Press 1982

All rights reserved. No part of this publication may be reproduced,
stored in a retrieval system, or transmitted, in any form or by any means,
electronic, mechanical, photocopying, recording, or otherwise, without
the prior permission of Oxford University Press

British Library Cataloguing in Publication Data
Benkovitz, Miriam J.
A bibliography of Ronald Firbank. — 2nd ed. —
(The Soho bibliographies; 16)
1. Firbank, Ronald — Bibliography
I. Title   II. Series
016.823'912   Z8298
ISBN 0-19-818188-4

Set by Hope Services, Abingdon
and printed in Great Britain
at the University Press, Oxford
by Eric Buckley
Printer to the University

To
MIRIAM JO
and ANNE

CONTENTS

INTRODUCTION TO THE SECOND EDITION — ix

INTRODUCTION — xii

A. Books and Pamphlets — 1

B. Contributions to Books — 67

C. Contributions to Periodicals — 79

Manuscripts and Typescripts — 85

APPENDIX: Supposititious Works — 95

ACKNOWLEDGMENTS — 99

INDEX — 101

INTRODUCTION TO THE SECOND EDITION

Ronald Firbank is 'alive & kicking'. That was how he described himself when, as a boy at school, he sent greetings to one of the family's servants. Now the phrase can be applied figuratively to Firbank and his literary well-being. Interest in Firbank persists, and information about him is constantly enlarging. Quite recently the Henry W. and Albert A. Berg Collection of The New York Public Library acquired hitherto unknown letters and documents which augment considerably the details of Firbank's relationship with his mother. On the one hand are Lady Firbank's frantic efforts to keep her son out of the army during the 1914-18 war and, on the other, their formal agreement for her tenancy of Denbigh Cottage at Richmond (from which he ejected Heather, his sister, after their mother's death).

More to the point here is the Berg Collection's acquisition of a typescript of *Concerning the Eccentricities of Cardinal Pirelli*. Indeed, the traffic in Firbankiana has affected this present edition a great deal. It has brought to light variant bindings for several titles as well as a first state of *The Flower Beneath the Foot*. Those plus translations of Firbank's novels into German, Dutch, and Italian and seven new titles have substantially expanded the first section of this edition, Section A, which lists books and pamphlets. The number of separate book publications is increased by ten.

Because Firbank made no direct contributions to books, Section B, which lists such contributions, was formerly left blank. Here it lists eleven books in which Firbank's letters, notebooks, and literary works are quoted. Doubtless there are inadvertent omissions from this section. The omission of doctoral dissertations is deliberate. After much reflec-

INTRODUCTION TO THE SECOND EDITION

tion, theses such as one by Otto Oppertshäuser published in Berlin in 1968, another by John Anthony Kiechler published in Bern in 1969, and a third by Jena Maes-Jelinek published in Paris in 1970 were not listed.

Similarly, articles derived from doctoral dissertations such as those by Rita Severi published in Italian journals are omitted. For other reasons, critical articles, however valuable and innovative — pieces by Carl Van Vechten, Edmund Wilson, Evelyn Waugh, and more recently Neville Braybrooke come to mind — are also excluded. Thus Section C, which lists contributions to periodicals, records only titles by Firbank. Section C has grown from nine to fourteen.

Perhaps the section which lists manuscripts and typescripts demonstrates most clearly how alive Ronald Firbank is. Besides the addition of the typescript of *Cardinal Pirelli*, at least two other typescripts, unknown in 1963, are listed here. But the most numerous changes shown in this section are changes in ownership and in the number of manuscripts and typescripts published. Both are sure indications of the vitality of interest in Firbank.

The sections named above correspond in order and in content with those of the first edition of *A Bibliography of Ronald Firbank*. Abbreviations and short titles in both editions are also identical, and an additional reference has been made to conform: the use of 'Columbia University' to mean The Rare Book and Manuscript Library of Columbia University. In other words, every effort has been made to retain the form and the concept of the first edition and to alter it only to expand its details.

For help in preparing this edition, I am grateful to the Albondocani Press, Arthur Barker Limited, the Henry W. and Albert A. Berg Collection of The New York Public Library, Mr George Bixby, British Broadcasting Corporation, The British Library, Mr John Byrne, Ms Carol S. Cerino, Mr Alan Clodd, Columbia University Libraries, The Library of Congress, Mr Robert Murray Davis, Mr Ed Drucker, Gerald Duckworth & Co. Ltd., Enitharmon Press,

INTRODUCTION TO THE SECOND EDITION

G. K. Hall & Co., Mr Frank W. Harrah, Sir Rupert Hart-Davis, Mr Brian Hill, Lord Horder, Humanities Research Library of the University of Texas, Miss Sonja P. Karsen, Mr Laurens van Krevelen, Mr Kenneth A. Lohf, Mr Barrie MacDonald, Mrs Phyllis Marchand, Meulenhoff Nederland BV, Winifred A. Myers (Autographs) Ltd., New Directions, Mr Otto Oppertshäuser, Ms Sybille Pantazzi, Mr Edward Potoker, Rizzoli Editore, Bertram Rota Ltd., Mrs Caroline Serotta, Ms Rita Severi, Mrs Ruth Clark Shepherd, Mr George F. Sims, Mrs Lola Szladits, and A. P. Watt & Son.

MIRIAM J. BENKOVITZ

Saratoga Springs, New York

INTRODUCTION

Ronald Firbank's concept of his work as art was not made up of the fiction alone. That was surely true after his Cambridge years when, sometime between mid-1909 and 1912 or 1913, Firbank deliberately set out to be a novelist and chose his undergraduate piece 'A Study in Opal' on which to build first *Vainglory* and ultimately, without exaggeration, his career as a writer. From that time, for Firbank, each novel had its separate artistic existence. Each began at least with the words and phrases and names tried out in his current notebook. Each achieved its own completeness with his careful approval of every detail of its publication.

Thus, this bibliography concerns itself with considerably more than the final stage of Firbank's works. Strictly speaking, the bibliography is based on the inspection and collation of at least six copies of first or special editions except for the one or two for which that number of copies could not be located after assiduous search. The vexatious problems of issues and states have not arisen, but care has been taken to distinguish between first impressions, called here first editions, and subsequent impressions. Contents of title-pages are reproduced without marking type sizes. Variant bindings, as detected, are listed even in the case of a unique copy, because it is significant in a consideration of Firbank's literary history. As for colours, their description has been kept as simple and as consistent as possible. No note is taken of the fact that the green stain on the top edge of many of Firbank's books regularly showed a wide and unpredictable range of hue within editions; throughout, the stain is simply called green.

Further details come from an investigation of the records of Firbank's publishers. In that connection it must be reported that Brentano's records no longer exist and that Grant Richards's office files, the property of the University

INTRODUCTION

of Texas, were not accessible. But by way of compensation the Library of the University of Illinois opened Richards's letter-books freely, New Directions was most helpful, and Gerald Duckworth and Company Ltd. was unstinting in response to numberless questions. The publishers' dates of release proved accurate enough in many cases to be accepted and so set down; in the event of doubt, a publication date is approximated usually from more than one source. The exact number of copies of each title delivered by the printer is stated. The production of dust-jackets has received attention, because they were important to Firbank.

Indeed, they were an essential part of the aesthetic image which Ronald Firbank had of his novels. Supervision of the design and printing of jackets, Firbank regarded as one of his rights — it was one way of getting value for money spent — as well as a responsibility. It was the same with frontispieces, illustrations, cloth, paper, printing, all the business of getting a novel produced. Attention to these things with each book meant to Firbank that he was finishing the job he had started even before he jotted down those words and phrases in his ubiquitous notebooks, when his novel was still 'radiantly unworded in ambitious conjecture'. Therefore, whenever available information makes it possible, this bibliography traces the development of each of Firbank's works from inception to publication.

In other words, no opportunity to enrich Firbank's literary history has been wilfully ignored. Consequently, many things which may appear to interpret the role of the bibliographer broadly are included. As an example, what Firbank called the sordid side of authorship, the financial side, is treated extensively, for it was an unending concern of his letters as early as those written in 1906 to Elkin Mathews. Even peripheral matters such as various playwrights' dramatizations of his works, successful and unsuccessful, are presented. Inevitably, some omissions occur. From Rome on 27 April 1924 Firbank wrote to his sister that he had been sent one of Carl Van Vechten's novels for review. The review has not been found. Possibly additional

INTRODUCTION

typescripts of the unpublished works 'The Mauve Tower' and 'True Love' exist; Ifan Kyrle Fletcher told of seeing them at Dulau's in Bond Street (*Ronald Firbank, A Memoir*, London, 1930, p. 24). No copies except those among the family papers have turned up. Furthermore, while Firbank's textual revisions are noted, detail is not provided on the grounds that to do so would amount to bibliographical licence. But every effort has been made to bear out Firbank's statement to his mother in a letter from Bordighera, dated 12 May [1923]: 'The more I think about my literary efforts in the light of others the less do I feel that I owe them any concession, either to happiness inspiration or money.'

Many facts were obtained from unpublished holograph letters. Quotations from Firbank letters are made by permission of Colonel Thomas Firbank and his solicitor Richard G. Medley of Field Roscoe & Co. The letters listed below have been cited with the further permission of their present owners:

Ronald Firbank to Lady Harriette Firbank	John F. Fleming
Ronald Firbank to Heather Firbank	Fales Collection, New York University Library
Ronald Firbank to Stuart Rose	Stuart Rose
Ronald Firbank to Carl Van Vechten	Henry W. and Albert A. Berg Collection of The New York Public Library and Carl Van Vechten

Unless otherwise designated in the text, the following letters are in my possession: Ronald Firbank to Grant Richards and George Wiggins, Lady Harriette Firbank to Grant Richards, and Albert Rutherston to Grant Richards. The Library of the University of Illinois and Bruce Harkness allowed inspection of Grant Richards's ledger and consented to citation from copies of letters in Richards's

INTRODUCTION

letter-books from Grant Richards and George Wiggins to Lady Harriette Firbank, Ronald Firbank, and others. I wish also to record permission to quote material in the files of the Society of Authors and to reproduce material published in the *Bulletin of The New York Public Library* and the *Papers of the Bibliographical Society of America*.

My indebtedness for help of many kinds is acknowledged elsewhere in this book. I want, however, to express a particular gratitude to Rupert Hart-Davis, whose interest and resourcefulness helped to surmount every difficulty, and to John D. Gordan and John Hayward, whose wisdom illumined the darkest problems. Special mention must be made, too, of the rare generosity of Nancy Cunard, Thomas Firbank, Bruce Harkness, Lord Horder, Stuart Rose, Donald G. Wing, and Carl Van Vechten. And my heartfelt thanks are due also to my colleagues Gladys M. Brownell, John P. Heins, and Mary Elizabeth Williams for services in the interest of bibliography too many to enumerate and to my parents for their patience with the litter of my papers and the noise of my typewriter.

MIRIAM J. BENKOVITZ

Skidmore College

A.
BOOKS AND PAMPHLETS

**A1 ODETTE D'ANTREVERNES AND 1905
A STUDY IN TEMPERAMENT**

a. First edition:

Odette D'Antrevernes | AND | A Study in Temperament | BY | ARTHUR FIRBANK | LONDON | ELKIN MATHEWS, VIGO STREET, W. | 1905

Crown 8°. $7\frac{1}{2}''\times 5\frac{5}{8}''$. 48 pp.
P. [1] half-title; p. [2] blank; p. [3] title; p. [4] blank; p. [5] fly-title; p. [6] blank; pp. [7]–27 text; p. [28] blank; p. [29] fly-title; p. [30] blank; pp. [31]–45 text; p. [46] imprint, 'PRINTED BY R. FOLKARD AND SON. 22, DEVONSHIRE STREET, | QUEEN SQUARE, LONDON, W.C.'; pp. [47–8] blank.

Issued simultaneously in sea-green stiff paper covers lettered in gilt or in rose stiff paper covers lettered in blue on upper cover: ARTHUR ANNESLEY RONALD FIRBANK | ODETTE D'ANTREVERNES | ONE FLORIN NET. Printed on white laid paper; top edges trimmed, other edges untrimmed.

Published June 1905 at 2s.; 500 copies were printed. Noted by *The Times Literary Supplement* 9 June 1905 under 'List of New Books and Reprints'. The British Library copy is dated 1 July 1905.

Both pieces in this volume were completed after January 1904. At the end of that month *A Study in Temperament* was still in progress. Firbank showed one version to R. St Clair Talboys, a schoolmaster then at Wellington College. And Talboys, in a letter of 24 January, wrote a long critique of the story, advised Firbank to read Hubert Crackanthorpe's 'Yew Trees and Peacocks' in *Sentimental Studies* before rewriting, and suggested the title for *A Study in Temperament*. (Unpublished letter, Miriam J. Benkovitz.) *Odette* was finished some time in September. Firbank's mother wrote on 25 September that she was 'so looking forward to tomorrow's post' because it might bring *Odette*; she promised to have it 'typewritten' at once and copies sent to her son, who was in Paris. (Unpublished letter, Berg Collection.)

Firbank had arranged for publication by mid-February 1905. Because wartime bombing destroyed Elkin Mathews's records, the exact terms of author–publisher agreement are unknown. Without doubt Firbank financed the production of his book. A publisher's statement dated 5 February 1906 and directed to Firbank at The Parsonage, Bielside, Aberdeenshire, where he was at school, showed 60 copies sold, with Elkin Mathews receiving 10 per cent on the first 26 and 5 per cent on the next 34.

A. BOOKS AND PAMPHLETS

b. Special large paper impression of Odette D'Antrevernes (1905):

Odette D'Antrevernes | BY | ARTHUR FIRBANK | LONDON | ELKIN MATHEWS, VIGO STREET, W. | 1905

Large demy 8°. $8\frac{5}{8}'' \times 6\frac{5}{8}''$. 26 pp.

P. [1] half-title; p. [2] blank; p. [3] title; p. [4] blank; pp. [5]-25 text; p. [26] blank.

Issued in cream vellum boards. Plate-marked and blocked in black on upper cover and along spine, upward: ODETTE. Printed on cream japanese vellum; six cream japanese vellum binder's leaves at front and seven at back plus two free endpapers each, front and back. On the verso of the first, top left, is the binder's stamp: BICKER'S & SON LEICESTER SQR. Recto of first endpaper and verso of last lined with beige silk moiré. All hinged to covers by a strip of cream kidskin, front and back. Covers lined with beige silk moiré ($7\frac{3}{4}'' \times 6''$). All edges trimmed; top edge gilt.

This impression consisted of ten copies for presentation by the author; none was for sale.

The half-title, p. [1], is the fly-title of the first *Odette* (A1a) differently imposed.

P. H. Muir ('A Bibliography of the First Editions of Books by Arthur Annesley Ronald Firbank [1886-1926]', Supplement to the *Bookman's Journal*, XV [1927], 3) calls this a special edition. But there can be no question of a separate edition, since the same setting (with one differently imposed preliminary and a corrected title) was used for both impressions.

To establish conclusive priority between the two is impossible. The peculiarities of the collation of the special impression (A^8, $B^4[B_4 + 1]$) as compared with that of the ordinary impression (A^8, BB_2-CC_2^8) weigh against these special copies as having precedence.

Firbank called them merely large paper copies of the first edition. In a letter to Carl Van Vechten from Fiesole, dated 3 May 1922, Firbank expressed surprise that his books, and especially *Odette*, were known in the United States. He added 'On my return to London in June I will try to find you a *first* edition. I have a few large paper copies... which were printed privately for me.'

From London on 29 June he wrote to tell Van Vechten that a copy had been sent,

> I have had quite a hunt for the child, & find that *ten* vellum-paper copies are all that Elkin Mathews ever did for me, & these having been given away (Queen Alexandra & the Infanta Isabella account for two), I send you *mine*, battered as it is. Please excuse the scars, etc., since the seven Adonises (to whom the others belong) refuse to part with *theirs* — at any rate the two whom I tried.

A. BOOKS AND PAMPHLETS

Firbank inscribed the book on the recto of the second binder's leaf: 'Presentation copy from Arthur Annesley Ronald Firbank to Carl Van Vechten Summer 1922 —.' This copy, which Van Vechten gave to the Berg Collection, is one of two available for examination, although a third copy, apparently uniform with the first, is noted.

The second available copy is also uniform with the first except in the following details. This copy measures $9'' \times 6\frac{3}{4}''$. The cream vellum binding is plate-marked and blocked in gilt on upper cover: ODETTE [*within a triple-rule frame*]; on lower cover: triple-rule frame; and on centre of spine upward: ODETTE [*within a single-rule frame*] with single rule at head and tail. An elaborate, gold-tooled inside border surrounds both silk paste-downs ($8\frac{1}{8}'' \times 5\frac{3}{4}'''$). There are five binder's leaves at front and six at back. This copy lacks the binder's stamp.

Perhaps this copy is one bound especially for Queen Alexandra. Laid in is a card ($3\frac{5}{8}'' \times 4\frac{3}{4}''$) with the royal coat of arms and WINDSOR CASTLE embossed in crimson. On the card is written in black ink, 'Book written by son of Sir J. Firbank M.P. aged 18. [*rule*] Thanked. 18 Nov 1905. L. G.'

A2   VAINGLORY   1915

a. First edition:

VAINGLORY | BY | RONALD FIRBANK | [*publisher's device*] | WITH A FRONTISPIECE BY | FELICIEN ROPS | LONDON | GRANT RICHARDS LTD. | ST MARTIN'S STREET | LEICESTER SQUARE | W. C.

Crown 8°. $7\frac{3}{8}'' \times 5''$. 264 pp., frontispiece, and 12-page publisher's catalogue inserted.

Pp. [1-2] blank; p. [3] half-title; p. [4] publisher's '*ANNOUNCEMENTS*' listing nine titles; frontispiece, colour process plate on white linen-finish coated paper (with protective tissue), tipped in facing p. [5]; p. [5] title; p. [6] imprint, 'PRINTED BY THE RIVERSIDE PRESS LIMITED | EDINBURGH | 1915', p. [7] fly-title; p. [8] blank; pp. 9-260 text; pp. [261-4] blank; 12-page publisher's catalogue with advertisements on pp. 1-7, preceded by unpaginated leaf with date, 'Spring 1915', publisher's monogram, name, and address on recto (verso blank) and followed by three unpaginated blank pages.

Issued in black cloth boards. Lettered in gilt on upper cover: VAINGLORY; across spine: VAIN- | GLORY | RONALD | FIRBANK | GRANT | RICHARDS. Printed on cream white laid paper; cream white wove endpapers of lighter stock. Top edge trimmed, stained green; other edges rough trimmed. White linen-finish coated paper dust-jacket lettered in black and decorated with a reproduction of

A. BOOKS AND PAMPHLETS

the frontispiece; the author's name appears on the jacket as A. A. R. Firbank.

Published 15 April 1915 at 6s.; 500 copies were printed. The British Library copy is dated 18 June 1915.

Some copies lack the publisher's catalogue.

Firbank offered *Vainglory* first to Martin Secker; he refused it but suggested that Grant Richards might be interested. Although Firbank called his book 'only thistledown' and a 'souflé', he said at the same time that 'nobody could guess of the sacrifice behind', and he wanted it published. So he took it to Richards. Richards read the manuscript during the Christmas week-end of 1914 and on Monday morning, 28 December, in a meeting with Firbank, explained the financial arrangements under which he would publish *Vainglory*. When Firbank left the publisher's office he took his manuscript with him, for no agreement had been reached. But later that same day Firbank wrote to say that he could not pay more than £80; if that sum, payable at once and the balance in April, was adequate, then he would return the copy of the book to Richards. (Unpublished letter, Library of University College London.) Consequently, Firbank signed an informal contract which Richards drew up on 29 December. By its terms Firbank agreed to pay £80 for the production and publication of 500 copies of *Vainglory* as nearly similar as possible in type, paper, and binding — the binding must be black, however, rather than dark red — to *The Hill of Dreams* by Arthur Machen. This amount was to cover every expense to the author except charges for correction of proofs. The agreement provided for an additional expenditure of £20 for advertising, 'especially in the "Morning Post" '. Firbank further agreed that this amount might be repaid Richards out of the first proceeds from sales; in the event sales did not realize £20, Firbank would not be expected to make up the difference. On all sales beyond that amount, except those to the author for his own use, the contract allowed Richards a commission of 10 per cent.

By 8 January, when he had approved a specimen page of the text and made a decision about the covers, Firbank was taking an active part in the book's production. 'That expression', he wrote to Richards, 'of not being able to "put a book down" I'm convinced has nothing to do with the inside.' (Copy of an unpublished letter, 25 January [1915], Library of University College London.) And he intended to make certain that his book 'be delightful to hold'. First, in accord with a suggestion by Richards, he required an illustration for frontispiece and dust-jacket. Since he could not arrange for one by Augustus John, Firbank settled on a Felicien Rops crayon-drawing already in his possession. The reproduction for *Vainglory* is the upper part of a coloured sketch showing a nude in a black hat. For the frontispiece and decoration on the jacket, Firbank consented to an outlay of £12. 17s. 6d. The position of the drawing on the page was a serious matter; 'everything', he told George Wiggins, Richards's manager, depended on 'hitting an effective position' on the paper.

A. BOOKS AND PAMPHLETS

Furthermore, Firbank was anxious lest the Rops drawing be mistaken for a Beardsley, because, as he wrote to Wiggins, there was an 'important nuance' between the two; to avoid confusion he urged that the artist be named on the dust-jacket. On the jacket, too, he wanted 'A. A. R. Firbank' instead of his Christian name; he told Wiggins, 'I feel sure that copies will sell better that way as one's acquaintance will recognise them sooner.' In both cases he wanted lettering with 'smartness & style'; he said he would be 'willingly Viennese just for once', and he named as a model the lettering on the cover of *Zuleika Dobson*. As for the dust-jacket's paper, he sent samples to Wiggins 'as a guide'; he found very smooth paper unpleasant but thought 'light rather coarse Venetian paper would be just the thing'. To Richards, Firbank sent a 'German book' with all edges stained green and suggested a similar treatment for his own book; green, he said, was 'quite a thrilling contrast' to the black covers. In the matter of proofs he grieved for his 'beautiful capital letters' removed by the printers, insisted on retaining those on pp. 49 and 179, and then sent instructions that the printers were not to 'replace any of those Capitals — they would not know where to put them & the result would be like almonds in a trifle'. (Copy of an unpublished letter, 25 January [1915], Library of University College London.) He had to have revises of the first two signatures and would have liked them for the entire book. But finally, on 31 March 1915 when he had seen a pre-publication copy, Firbank wrote to Richards, 'A line to tell you how delighted I am with Vainglory. In such charming looks who could have the heart to be horrid.' (Unpublished letter, Alan Anderson.)

However pleased Firbank was with the book, its binding did not do for himself and his mother. Lady Firbank took an active interest in *Vainglory*. She urged Richards to make certain that it was 'well reviewed', and she induced W. H. Smith & Son to order copies for their stalls and shops. Her recompense was a specially bound copy of *Vainglory*. Firbank arranged for two such copies, one for her and one for himself: a white vellum binding for two copies is noted. Both are platemarked and blocked in gilt at the top left corner of the upper cover: VAINGLORY; and along the spine, upward: VAINGLORY — RONALD FIRBANK. On one copy a typographic ornament, platemarked and blocked in gilt, follows the title on the upper cover. In both copies all edges are trimmed and the top edge is gilt. Both volumes further differ from the ordinary one (A2a) in that they measure $7\frac{3}{16}''\times 4\frac{3}{8}''$, their first leaf is a binder's leaf, and the first signature lacks the first two leaves (A^{8-2}, B-Q^8, R4). In both copies, pp. [1-4] are blank; thus both lack the half-title and publisher's announcements; their last leaf is a binder's leaf; and both lack the publisher's catalogue. The binder's leaves and endpapers are identical with the text paper. The copy without the typographic ornament on the upper cover was a gift from the author to his mother and is inscribed to her, 'For darling Baba from Artie 1918'.

A. BOOKS AND PAMPHLETS

It is contained with uniformly bound copies of *Inclinations* (A3) and *Caprice* (A5) in a vellum slip case.

The copy with the typographic ornament on the upper cover was the author's and doubtless once among the published works and manuscripts which Osbert Sitwell observed in Firbank's rooms opposite Magdalen Tower, Oxford (cf. *Noble Essences*, London, 1950, p. 73). On the upper board-paper the author wrote with pencil, 'Ronald Firbank 78 Brook Street'. Throughout he made numerous holograph revisions in purple ink. With one exception these revisions were included in the American edition (A2b).

The exception is the deletion, indicated everywhere, of the name Winsome and the substitution for it of Sacheverell. This was Firbank's proposed retaliation for an incident which occurred in Rome in late October 1923. He wrote his mother that when he lunched with Lord Berners at his home in Rome, they discussed a plaster cast of a Psyche in one of Berners's sitting-rooms and agreed it was 'a horror'. Apparently at another luncheon party the next day Berners again 'deplored the cast of Psyche saying "What am I going to do with it?" ' Firbank's account continues,

> one of the Sitwells said 'Send it to Ronald!' This amused everybody, & on the broken crown of the Psyche the whole luncheon party autographed their names thus
>
> 'Homage to Ronald Firbank from Berners, Edith Sitwell, Sacheverell Sitwell, Geoffrey Lovelace (the little artist) Aldous Huxley, Moira [Maria] Huxley, Harold Nicholson, Vita Sackville West . . . , W. T. Walton, & Evan [Morgan].'

Although he thought the spectacle of Lord Berners's butler delivering the statue in a cab laughable, Firbank 'naturally took offence'. That was true even though the episode hardly surprised him; he had already told his mother that all the English in Rome were 'jealous & spiteful', that Rome might well be Oxford as far as ' "the collony" go'. This attitude was kept alive by the maliciously funny reports which Geoffrey Lovelace brought him almost every day of their stay in Rome. In any case Firbank had a particular distrust of Sacheverell Sitwell and had had since 1919 when, in Oxford, he accused Sitwell of insincerity and gossip. Thus some months after the Berners incident, as he revised *Vainglory*, he substituted Sacheverell for Winsome. Then Firbank reconsidered, and to emphasize that he did not want the change he wrote on the recto of the first free endpaper: 'N.B. "Sacheverell" = retain "Winsome" throughout — Retain name Winsome NOT Sacheverell as alternate.'

b. *First American edition* (1925):

VAINGLORY | BY | RONALD FIRBANK | [*orange, diamond shaped publisher's device in blind stamped diamond*

A. BOOKS AND PAMPHLETS

panel] | NEW YORK | BRENTANO'S | PUBLISHERS
Crown 8°. $7\frac{3}{8}''\times 4\frac{7}{8}''$. [iv], 256 pp., and frontispiece.

P. [i] half-title; p. [ii] blank; frontispiece, reproduction by colour process plate of Rops's drawing as used in first edition (A2a) on white coated paper (with protective tissue), tipped in facing p. [iii]; p. [iii] title; p. [iv] copyright notice and below $\frac{5}{16}''$ rule, reservation of rights and imprint, 'PRINTED IN THE UNITED STATES OF AMERICA'; pp. 1–249 text; pp. [250–6] blank. A blank page occurs at the end of some chapters, that is pp. [64], [92], [108], [126], [170], [182], [192], [200], [216], [236], [242].

Issued in black cloth boards. Lettered in gilt on upper cover VAINGLORY; across spine: VAINGLORY | RONALD | FIRBANK | BRENTANO'S. Printed on cream white laid paper; cream white wove endpapers. Top edge trimmed, stained green; other edges rough trimmed. White linen-finish coated paper dust-jacket lettered in rose, light blue, and black and decorated with half-tone reproduction in colour of illustration signed in the plate: Joseph Fannell.

Published October or November 1925 at $2; the number of copies printed cannot be ascertained. Noted by *New York Post*, 16 October 1925, in 'Books on Our Table'; *The New York Times Book Review*, 18 October 1925, in 'Latest Books'; and *Publishers' Weekly*, 28 November 1925. Brentano's named 8 October 1925 as publication date on its application for copyright. The Library of Congress copy is dated 10 October 1925.

The agreement for publication is dated 14 October 1925.

The text is a revised version of the first edition (A2a). According to his correspondence with Stuart Rose of Brentano's, Firbank devoted less than a month in early 1925 to making the revisions. The frontispiece was printed from the original colour-blocks, which Richards sent to Brentano's.

At least one subsequent impression was issued in November 1925, and there may have been still another. Firbank wrote from Cairo on 20 February 1926: 'Vainglory (published Oct) in America is now in its third edition (15000).' No copy of the third impression has been located. The second is uniform with the first except that it lacks the frontispiece and has on p. [iv] a notice of both printings. It was issued in tan cloth boards lettered in black on the upper cover within a single-rule black frame: VAINGLORY, and across the spine: VAINGLORY | BRENTANO'S with a black rule at head and tail.

A3   INCLINATIONS   1916

First edition:

INCLINATIONS | BY | RONALD FIRBANK | AUTHOR OF "VAINGLORY" | [*publisher's device*] | With Two

A. BOOKS AND PAMPHLETS

Drawings by Albert Rutherston (Rothenstein) | LONDON | GRANT RICHARDS LTD. | ST MARTIN'S STREET | LEICESTER SQUARE | MDCCCCXVI

Crown 8°. $7\frac{7}{16}''$ × 5". 200 pp., frontispiece, and 8-page publisher's catalogue inserted.

Pp. [1-2] blank; p. [3] half-title; p. [4] blank; frontispiece, black and white collotype within single-rule black frame on calendered cream white paper (with protective tissue), tipped in facing p. [5]; p. [5] title; p. [6] imprint, 'PRINTED BY THE RIVERSIDE PRESS LIMITED | EDINBURGH'; p. [7] divisional fly-title; p. [8] epigraph; pp. 9-147 text; p. [148] blank; p. [149] divisional fly-title; p. [150] epigraph; pp. 151-200 text; on p. 200 is a tail-piece produced in black and white line; 8-page publisher's catalogue with date, 'Spring 1916', publisher's monogram, name, and address on p. [1], advertisements on pp. 2-7, and p. [8] blank.

Issued in black cloth boards. Lettered in gilt on upper cover: INCLINATIONS; across spine: INCLIN- | ATIONS | RONALD | FIRBANK | GRANT | RICHARDS. Printed on cream white laid paper, cream white wove endpapers of lighter stock. Top edge trimmed, stained green; other edges rough trimmed. White linen-finish coated paper dust-jacket lettered in black and decorated with half-tone reproduction in colour of frontispiece. The dust-jacket is noteworthy in that the lettering on its spine reads A. A. R. | Firbank | Author of | "Vainglory" whereas Firbank's name appears elsewhere in *Inclinations* and in all subsequent publications as Ronald Firbank.

Published 17 June 1916 at 6s.; 500 copies were printed. The British Library copy is dated 2 February 1917.

Some copies lack the publisher's catalogue.

All copies of the first edition contain a cancel title-leaf inserted with its integral leaf (pp. 11 and 12) for sewing at the bindery. On 1 June 1916 Wiggins sent the binding order for *Inclinations* to James Burn and Company Ltd with a letter which said in part, 'You cannot sew the books as there will be a four page cancel title to be *sewn* in. This will be coming to you from the Riverside Press.' The cancel was necessitated by difficulties which arose at some time after 16 March and before 19 April, when the artist engaged to design the frontispiece, tail-piece, and dust-jacket changed his name from Albert Rothenstein to Albert Rutherston. He wanted his name to appear as Rutherston on the title-page, and he lettered it that way in his design for the jacket. Firbank objected; he insisted that the public would not recognize the new name. In a letter to Grant Richards dated 21 May 1916 Firbank wrote that unless Rutherston were willing to have his original name on the title-page, it had better be left off entirely. If neither alternative proved agreeable to the artist, then Firbank declared he would exchange the drawings for the fee paid. To retain the drawings and leave off the artist's name was out of the question. Rutherston had told Richards in a letter of 16 March, 'With regard to my name, I think it must appear on the Title Page. . . . I feel that Firbank is scarcely a writer of sufficient weight or name for me to have drawings in the book unannounced.' As for returning the drawings, that meant renewed problems for Richards: at the author's suggestion he had already instructed the printer to lop a few of the final pages so as to bring the page-count from 199 to 200, and the tail-piece was needed to balance the last page. Richards worked out a compromise whereby the title-page was reprinted to include both names of the artist, but the jacket went unchanged with his name as Rutherston.

This situation was only one of several which harassed Firbank in the publication of *Inclinations*. When he gave the typescript of all but the last chapter to Richards on 17 January 1916 he did so reluctantly. 'I am afraid I have hurried & spoilt my book', he wrote, 'although I can make it quite complete by compression.' Richards wanted it for his spring list, however, and on 20 January 1916 he and Firbank entered into an agreement for the production of 500 copies of *Inclinations* on the same terms as *Vainglory*; that is a cost to Firbank of £80 and a return of proceeds from sales less 10 per cent. The expense of the illustrations and jacket came to an additional £21.18s. Meanwhile Firbank managed with hard work to complete the last chapter so that it went to the printer on 21 January. Then, after all his haste, he received no proofs. By letter and telegram he demanded them throughout February and most of March. At last they came, but he made so many corrections that he required proofs a second time. Typically his punctuation concerned him, and he complained about the printers, 'They have dressed me out in armour — far too much. By changing the punctuation all "goes". Since one never attempted to be classic — . . . I feel like "a waiter" in evening-dress!' But before revised proofs could be supplied, the printers went on strike. He told Richards, 'This long delay with the printers & my hurried ending go so badly together — Had I forseen a "strike" I would have been more "mature"! . . . I feel so ashamed of my flimsy endings & all the heavy Time!' Although Richards advised against any changes, Firbank asked as late as 28 May whether 'weary fingers' at the top of p. 22 could be altered to 'psychic fingers'. Furthermore, he wanted all edges of the book stained 'a very fascinating shade of pink rather brilliant and yet quite subdued to give a value to the black boards', and suggested a malmaison as a guide to the colour. It was too late for textual revision, and a satisfactory pink was never achieved.

A white vellum binding for two copies is noted. Both are plate-marked and blocked in gilt at the top left corner of the upper cover: INCLINATIONS; and along the spine, upward: INCLINATIONS — RONALD FIRBANK. On one copy a typographic ornament, plate-marked and blocked in gilt, follows the title on the upper cover. Both volumes further differ from the ordinary one (A3) in that they measure $7\frac{3}{16}'' \times 4\frac{13}{16}''$; all edges are trimmed and the top edge is gilt; their

A. BOOKS AND PAMPHLETS

first and last leaves are binder's leaves and both lack the publisher's catalogue. Binder's leaves and endpapers are cream white laid paper watermarked with a large, decorative fleur-de-lis. The copy without the typographic ornament on the upper cover was a gift from the author to his mother and is inscribed to her 'With love from Artie, 1918.' It is contained with uniformly bound copies of *Vainglory* (A2a) and *Caprice* (A5) in a vellum slip-case. The copy with the typographic ornament was the author's copy.

A4   ODETTE A FAIRY TALE FOR   1916
                   WEARY PEOPLE

First separate illustrated edition:

ODETTE | A FAIRY TALE FOR WEARY PEOPLE | BY | RONALD FIRBANK | WITH FOUR ILLUSTRATIONS | BY ALBERT BUHRER | LONDON | GRANT RICHARDS LIMITED | ST. MARTIN'S STREET | 1916

4°. 8" × 6". 40 pp. (unpaginated).

P. [1] half-title; p. [2] list of works '*BY THE SAME AUTHOR*'; p. [3] blank; p. [4] frontispiece, a black and white line cut on text paper with legend, 'AVE MARIA'; p. [5] title; p. [6] blank; p. [7] dedication, '*IN ALL THE WORLD | TO | THE DEAREST OF MOTHERS*'; p. [8] blank; pp. [9-39] text; p. [40] imprint, 'GARDEN CITY | PRESS LTD., | :: PRINTERS, :: | LETCHWORTH.' Three illustrations in the text produced uniformly with the frontispiece are printed on text paper with legends: 'THE NURSE'S STORY' p. [15]. 'THE ROSE GARDEN' p. [21], 'BOIS=FLEUR' p. [31]. Pp. [16], [22], [32] are blank. A decorative initial letter produced in line commences each of the three divisions of the text, pp. [9], [18], [24].

Issued in beige stiff paper covers, $8\frac{5}{16}"$ × $6\frac{3}{16}"$. Lettered in black on upper cover: ODETTE | *A Fairy Tale for* | *Weary People* | [*frontispiece reproduced in three colour line cut but lacking legend*] | By | RONALD FIRBANK | ONE SHILLING NET; along spine upward: ODETTE: *A Fairy Tale for Weary People* By RONALD FIRBANK; on lower cover is a black and white vignette produced in line. Printed on cream laid paper watermarked: ANTIQUE DE LUXE; cream laid endpapers. One leaf of each endpaper is inserted under the folding flaps of the covers. Top edge trimmed; other edges rough trimmed.

Published 13 December 1916 at 1*s*.; 2,000 copies were printed, of which Firbank reserved 20 for gifts. The British Library reports its copy as lost.

The text is a slightly revised version of the 1905 edition (A1a). Firbank made the changes so that the 'Richards Odette', as he told

A. BOOKS AND PAMPHLETS

Carl Van Vechten in a letter dated 22 June [1922], would be 'less naif' than the earlier one.

The memorandum of agreement, dated 18 July 1916, stipulated for the production of 2,000 copies of *Odette* with illustrations and decorated covers at a cost to Firbank of £65; Richards's commission amounted to 15 per cent of sales. After Richards urged it, Firbank grudgingly authorized another £2. 2s. — a total of £12. 12s. — paid the artist for 'a great deal more work on the drawings than he had expected to do'.

Firbank was as attentive to details in the publication of *Odette* as he had been in that of his earlier books, for as always he longed for his book 'to be really captivating & lovely'. He began by suggesting Alastair as the illustrator, because he was 'sufficiently Catholic . . . might be thrilling' and could give the book 'a Gothic air — Tres "St Sulpice"'. But Firbank was wholly receptive to the artist engaged by Richards, Albert Buhrer, who at that time often signed his work Tell and later called himself Adrian Bury. Firbank liked Buhrer's drawings, and after much consideration and several letters to Richards and Wiggins wrote the legends and decided on the colour of the illustration on the upper cover. The matter of the vignette for the lower cover, however, was most vexing. In July Firbank thought of 'a distant scene of Tours. . . . Something all towers & spires & a good round dome for S^t. Martin's! The Cathedral has twin-towers . . . & the Loire sails by under 3 stone bridges amid sand-reefs & Poplars —.' But in October he had several other ideas: 'a garland of thorns & Roses — Otherwise a small drawing of a Dove descending — or a Madonna Lilly or two or some little old-world flower — such as a pansy — but the crown of thorns with a "Martyr's" face inside would be *irresistible* & suit the book —.' Then he puzzled over the title, whether 'A Fairy Tale for Weary People' was preferable to 'Odette: A Fairy Tale for Weary People'. It was Firbank who decreed that the book have no pagination, for he found unnumbered pages 'more restful'. As usual he was impatient for publication. On 26 November 1916 he urged Richards to bring out *Odette* at once; he wrote saying that as the drawings were all dated 1916, the book would very likely be dismissed as ' "last year's goods" ' within a week or two after its appearance. And he was anxious that it go out extensively for review. 'Never again', he told Richards, 'will I be so respectable I fear.'

A variant binding state for twelve copies is noted. These were produced by order of the author's mother, Lady Firbank, in 1920. On 20 July 1920 Richards sent her a specimen of the 'style of binding' he proposed to use. And on 10 August he delivered the twelve specially bound copies. No example of this variant binding has been positively identified, but it may be one of white buckram boards, 8" × 6", lettered in gilt on the upper cover: ODETTE D'ANTRE-VERNES | RONALD FIRBANK. Two copies in such a binding are noted. Both copies, 32 pp. (unpaginated), lack frontispiece and

A. BOOKS AND PAMPHLETS

illustrations, having only stubs of the leaves on which these were printed. One of these copies, a part of the Jack H. Samuels Library, Columbia University Library, bears the holograph inscription, 'To his Eminence, Cardinal Archbishop of Seville, from his devoted servant the Author —.'

This book was a favourite of Lady Firbank. The author told Van Vechten in a letter from Fiesole dated 3 May 1922 that *Odette* had been reprinted to please his mother. And immediately after Richards published it she wrote to tell him how much she liked the new edition and to remark on the story's 'exquisite feeling & beauty'. At the end of January 1917 Firbank sent Richards his mother's idea for an Easter version.

In late 1920 the author's sister, Heather Firbank, translated *Odette* into German. Fragments of her holograph manuscript were among the family papers. Three years later she made a translation into Italian. This manuscript, dated April 1923, consists of 45 leaves; it is a part of the Berg Collection. Neither translation was published.

A5 CAPRICE 1917

First edition:

CAPRICE | BY | RONALD FIRBANK | [*publisher's device*] | With a Frontispiece by Augustus John | LONDON | GRANT RICHARDS LTD. | ST MARTIN'S STREET | LEICESTER SQUARE | MDCCCCXVII

Crown 8°. $7\frac{3}{8}'' \times 5''$. 144 pp. and frontispiece.

Pp. [1-2] blank; p. [3] half-title; p. [4] list of works 'BY THE SAME AUTHOR'; frontispiece, half-tone in colour on white linen-finish coated paper (with protective tissue), tipped in facing p. [5]; p. [5] title; p. [6] imprint, 'PRINTED IN GREAT BRITAIN BY | THE GARDEN CITY PRESS LTD., LETCHWORTH'; p. [7] dedication, 'TO | STEPHEN HAMMERTON |, Τίς δ' ἀγροιῶτίς τοι θέλγει νόον, | οὐκ ἐπισταμένα τὰ βράκε 'ελκην ἐπὶ τῶν σφύρων. — Sappho.'; p. [8] blank; pp. 9-141 text; pp. [142-4] blank.

Issued in black cloth boards. Lettered in gilt on upper cover: CAPRICE; across spine: CAPRICE | RONALD | FIRBANK | GRANT | RICHARDS. Printed on cream white laid paper; cream white laid endpapers. Top edge trimmed, stained green; other edges rough trimmed. White linen-finish coated paper dust-jacket lettered in black and decorated with a reproduction of the frontispiece within a single-rule black frame on three sides and ruled block at foot of jacket.

Published November 1917 at 5s.; 500 copies were printed. The publisher's records name 17 October as date of issue, but the release

A. BOOKS AND PAMPHLETS

date was some weeks later. On 16 October Richards sent out three 'early copies got very specially' to satisfy Firbank's 'desire to have the book ready on the 17th'. Noted by *The Bookseller* in 'Alphabetical List of Principal Publications for November 1917' and *Town Topics*, 23 November 1917. The British Library copy is dated 21 January 1918.

Although by 25 August 1916 Firbank asked that *Caprice* be announced in *Odette* as 'in preparation', he did not show the typescript to Richards until 19 June 1917. Then he did so with apprehension; 'I fear you will find Caprice "nothing" ', he told Richards and added that much revision was needed.

But Richards had long been eager for the book, and three days later, on 22 June, he sent Firbank a memorandum of agreement. This provided for an edition of 500 copies in the same form as that of *Inclinations*, but without frontispiece or jacket, at a cost to the author of £70. An illustration cost Firbank £25 and its production for frontispiece and dust-jacket another £21. In return he was to receive proceeds of sale less a 10 per cent commission payable to Richards. Richards agreed to forfeit £10 if the book were not published by the end of October so long as the author kept the first proofs no more than two weeks, and the second proofs one week. Printer's charges for corrections to proofs and additions were Firbank's responsibility.

The publication of *Caprice* marked the first difference between Richards and Firbank. The book's production went smoothly. Had John not agreed to do the frontispiece, Firbank had in mind A. H. Fish (Richards's suggestion), William Strang, or Althea Giles. But in spite of allusions in the text, later removed, which Firbank feared might offend him, John provided a drawing and selected its colours, blue on cream. Problems arose over Firbank's spelling of Tybalt and Tchekov, but these were quickly settled. His insistence on having the book ready by 17 October was satisfied by pre-publication copies. Then in an informal advertisement which appeared in the 25 October 1917 issue of the *Times Literary Supplement*, Richards described *Caprice* as 'like nothing else on earth'. The author and his mother were affronted. Richards wrote at least two letters to defend himself and his advertisement. He maintained that the phrase was applicable to *Caprice* in the same way as it might be to 'some of the greatly admired paintings by the very modern men'; he thought no one would have objected to the word unique; and he pointed out that the advertisement had interested G. P. Putnam's Sons enough to ask whether they might consider the book for America.

Putnam's decided against publication. Brentano's, New York, reached the same decision some eight years later, early in 1925. In November or December 1924 Stuart Rose, acting for Brentano's, suggested an American edition with a new preface. Firbank agreed to write the preface in a letter from Rome dated 16 December 1924, and on 16 February 1925 he sent it to Rose. Then Brentano's resolved

A. BOOKS AND PAMPHLETS

not to publish. Firbank told Van Vechten, 'I was very disappointed Brentano's did not go ahead with Caprice after hustling as I did with the preface! . . . I fear it shocked them.'

A white vellum binding for two copies is noted. Both are plate-marked and blocked in gilt at the top left corner of the upper cover: CAPRICE; and along the spine, upward: CAPRICE – RONALD FIRBANK. On one copy a typographic ornament, plate-marked and blocked in gilt, follows the title on the upper cover. Both volumes further differ from the ordinary one (A5) in that they measure $7\frac{3}{16}'' \times 4\frac{3}{4}''$; all edges are trimmed and the top edge is gilt; pp. [3] and [4] are blank, and both have a final binder's leaf. The binder's leaf and endpapers are cream white laid paper watermarked with a large decorative fleur-de-lis. The copy with the typographic ornament was the author's copy. The second copy was a gift from the author to his mother and is inscribed to her, 'For darling Baba 1918'. It is contained with uniformly bound copies of *Vainglory* (A2) and *Inclinations* (A3) in a vellum slip-case.

Caprice as adapted for broadcasting and produced by Douglas Cleverdon was presented on the Third Programme of the British Broadcasting Corporation on 25 February 1957 and again on 27 February.

A6   VALMOUTH   1919

a. First edition:

VALMOUTH | A ROMANTIC NOVEL | BY | RONALD FIRBANK | AUTHOR OF "VAINGLORY" | [*publisher's device*] | WITH A FRONTISPIECE BY | AUGUSTUS JOHN | LONDON | GRANT RICHARDS LTD. | ST MARTIN'S STREET | 1919

Crown 8°. $7\frac{5}{16}'' \times 4\frac{13}{16}''$. 212 pp. and frontispiece.

P. [1] half-title; p. [2] blank; frontispiece, half-tone in colour on white linen-finish coated paper (with protective tissue), tipped in facing p. [3]; p. [3] title; p. [4] imprint, 'PRINTED IN GREAT BRITAIN BY THE RIVERSIDE PRESS LIMITED | EDINBURGH'; p. [5] fly-title; p. [6] blank; pp. 7-209 text; pp. [210-12] blank.

Issued in black cloth boards. Lettered in gilt on upper cover: VALMOUTH; across spine: VALMOUTH | RONALD | FIRBANK | GRANT | RICHARDS. Printed on cream white wove paper; cream white wove endpapers of lighter stock. Top edge trimmed, stained green; other edges rough trimmed. White linen-finish coated paper dust-jacket lettered in black and decorated with reproduction of frontispiece within a single-rule black frame on three sides and ruled block at foot of jacket.

A. BOOKS AND PAMPHLETS

Published 17 November 1919 at 6s.; 500 copies were printed. The British Library copy is dated 12 December 1919.

By 1 July 1917, less than ten days after he had arranged for the publication of *Caprice*, Firbank had started *Valmouth*. Though he considered it 'wonderful' to have survived his several books 'written on other peoples tables & other peoples chairs', he told Richards it would be his last — and his best. At that time he thought of calling it either 'The Centenarians of Glennyfurry' or 'Glennyfurry: A Romance', and it was announced in *Caprice* as 'Glenmouth: A Romantic Novel'.

Richards and Firbank concluded the memorandum for *Valmouth*'s publication on 10 July 1919. Firbank agreed to pay the cost of producing an edition of 500 copies plus 25 per cent, an amount that totalled £116. 6s. 2d.; he was responsible for the cost of all revisions and advertisements. In return he received the proceeds of sales less a 15 per cent commission payable to Richards.

Firbank's first idea for a frontispiece was a 'Gauguin negress', but finding anything from which to make a suitable reproduction proved impossible. Meanwhile he saw a drawing in black and white 'of a lady in eighteenth century dress' on the mantelpiece in Augustus John's Mallord Street studio, and he secured that for both frontispiece and decoration on the jacket.

Valmouth was the first of Firbank's books offered for sale in Australia.

A white vellum binding for one copy is noted. It is plate-marked and blocked in gilt at the top left corner of the upper cover: VALMOUTH [*typographic ornament*]; and along the spine upward: VALMOUTH — RONALD FIRBANK. The volume further differs from the ordinary one (A6a) in that it measures $7\frac{3}{16}'' \times 4\frac{7}{8}''$; all edges are trimmed and the top edge is gilt; its first and last leaves are binder's leaves and the last signature lacks the last leaf (A–N^8, O$^{2-1}$). Binder's leaves and endpapers are cream white wove paper watermarked with a monogram and 'Baskerville Vellum Wove'.

On 5 May 1926 Brentano's opened negotiations with Firbank for an American edition; publication was set for October. No agreement had been concluded when Firbank died on 21 May. Brentano's were still trying to get the necessary authorization in August, but Firbank's solicitors did not grant it.

Sandy Wilson presented a musical comedy adaptation of *Valmouth* with Bertice Reading as Mrs Yajñavalkya, Fenella Fielding as Lady Parvula, and Doris Hare as Granny Tooke at the New Shakespeare Theatre, Liverpool, on 16 September 1958. The show opened in London at the Lyric Theatre, Hammersmith, on 2 October. On 27 January 1959 it moved to the West End, where it played at the Saville Theatre. There Cleo Laine replaced Miss Reading. The musical numbers were recorded on the Pye label, and the Noel Gay Music Company, London, published the music for four selections.

A. BOOKS AND PAMPHLETS

Mr Wilson's musical comedy version opened in New York on 6 October 1960 for a run of fourteen performances. This was an off-Broadway presentation of Gene Andrewski and Associates at the York Playhouse. Miss Reading was again in the leading role.

b. Illustrated edition, English issue (1956):

RONALD FIRBANK | [*five pointed star*] | VALMOUTH | With illustrations by | PHILIPPE JULLIAN | [*floral drawing produced in black and white line*] | GERALD DUCKWORTH & CO. LTD. | 3 *Henrietta Street*, London, W.C.2

Demy 8°. $8\frac{7}{16}'' \times 5\frac{1}{2}''$. 128 pp., frontispiece, and 7 illustrations.

P. [1] half-title; p. [2] blank; frontispiece, line cut in colour on text paper sewed, facing p. [3]; p. [3] title; p. [4] publication note and imprint, 'PRINTED IN GREAT BRITAIN BY | WILLMER BROTHERS AND COMPANY LIMITED, BIRKENHEAD'; pp. 5–127 text with vignettes, black and white line cuts, at head of all chapters and at foot of some; p. [128] blank. Illustrations, line cuts in colour on text paper, facing pp. 14, 32, 40, 46, 62, 80, 126; all are tipped in except that facing p. 14, which is on the recto of a leaf conjugate with the frontispiece leaf and sewed.

Issued in mauve cloth boards. Blocked in gilt on upper cover: facsimile of author's early signature, A. A. R Firbank; across spine: V | A | L | M | O | U | T | H | DUCKWORTH. Printed on white wove paper; white wove endpapers. All edges trimmed; top edge stained mauve. Pink paper dust-jacket printed in black and decorated with reproduction in black and green of multi-colour illustration facing p. 40.

Published 5 July 1956 at 21*s.*; 2,500 copies were printed, of which 250 were for export to America.

The text is that of *The Works* (A12a).

c. Illustrated edition, American issue (1956):

The American issue consisted of imported bound copies with uniform title-leaf except for a label ($\frac{3}{4}'' \times 3\frac{1}{2}''$) printed in black on white coated paper, 'NEW DIRECTIONS | 333 Sixth Avenue, New York 14, N.Y.', pasted over the Duckworth name and address p. [3]. The label is pasted over the Duckworth name and address on the lower dust-jacket also; the shilling price printed on the jacket is clipped, and the dollar price stamped in.

Published 1 November 1956 at $4.25; 250 copies were issued.

A. BOOKS AND PAMPHLETS

A7   THE PRINCESS ZOUBAROFF   1920

First edition:

THE PRINCESS | ZOUBAROFF | [*illustration, half-tone in colour within single-rule black frame*] | A COMEDY BY RONALD FIRBANK | WITH FRONTISPIECE AND DECORATION BY MICHEL SEVIER | LONDON: GRANT RICHARDS LIMITED 1920

Crown 8°. $7\frac{3}{8}'' \times 4\frac{7}{8}''$. 120 pp. and conjugate frontispiece and title leaves.

Pp. [1-2] blank; p. [3] half-title; p. [4] blank; frontispiece, half-tone in colour within $\frac{1}{8}''$ single-rule gilt frame (with protective tissue), and title on verso and recto respectively (reverse sides blank) of white linen-finish coated paper conjugate leaves tipped in between pp. [4] and [5]; p. [5] fly-title; p. [6] list of 'DRAMATIC PERSONÆ'; pp. 7-112 text and below $1\frac{3}{4}''$ rule at foot of p. 112 imprint, 'PRINTED IN GREAT BRITAIN BY THE RIVERSIDE PRESS LIMITED | EDINBURGH'; pp. [133-18], with p. [114] blank, integral catalogue of 'OTHER BOOKS BY | RONALD FIRBANK'; pp. [119-20] blank.

Issued in black cloth boards. Lettered in gilt on upper cover: THE PRINCES | ZOUBAROFF; across spine: THE | PRINCESS | ZOU-BAROFF | RONALD | FIRBANK | GRANT | RICHARDS. Printed on cream white laid paper; cream white wove endpapers of lighter stock. Top edge trimmed, stained green; other edges rough trimmed. White linen-finish coated paper dust-jacket lettered in black and decorated with reproduction of frontispiece within single-rule black frame on three sides and ruled block at foot of jacket.

Published 26 November 1920 at 6s.; 530 copies were printed but, according to the Grant Richards ledger, only 513 were bound. The British Library copy is dated 1 January 1921.

The British Library copy lacks the fly-title leaf, having only the naked stub. All copies offered for sale contain a cancel fly-title leaf pasted to the stub. On the recto of the cancelland was the dedication, 'To the Hon. Evan Morgan in Souvenir Amicale of a "Previous Incarnation".' The dedication was suppressed in this way:

Richards planned to publish on 8 November 1920, one of three days in November which Firbank called 'lucky'. By 3 November 300 copies were bound, and Richards gave one to the artist Michel Sevier. Sevier showed it to several friends, one of whom was Evan Morgan. The next morning the publisher learned from Morgan that he 'strongly objected to being made the recipient of the dedication'. According to Richards, Morgan was 'truculent', he talked about ' "highly placed personages" at St. James's Palace on whom he was in waiting, and generally tried to ride about three horses at once'. Richards explained his inability to cancel the page without instructions from Firbank, then travelling in North Africa; furthermore, the fact that the dedication leaf immedately followed the conjugate frontispiece and title leaves occasioned unusual technical problems. Richards lent Morgan a copy in the hope that when he had read it he would withdraw his objections. But the book was returned through Morgan's solicitors, Peacock and Goddard, whose accompanying letter dated 4 November 1920 emphasized their client's resentment at being 'associated with the book in any way especially having regard to its general tone towards the Catholic Church of which he is a member'. The letter added that if the book appeared with the dedication, Morgan would 'take such steps as he may be advised to protect his interests and to make his views on the subject perfectly clear to the public and his friends'. Richards moved the publication date to Firbank's next lucky day, 13 November, and wrote to Peacock and Goddard pleading Morgan's earlier consent to the dedication, Firbank's absence from England, his own obligations, technical difficulties, and a probable expense of 'something in the neighbourhood of fifty pounds'. He failed to move the solicitors. Meanwhile, without an exact address for Firbank, Richards sent him several harried letters.

Apparently none of these reached Firbank until 11 November; on the 9th he wrote to his mother that he believed his play had been published the day before. When he did receive Richards's letter, by his own statement, Firbank acted at once: 'I wired that on no account would I dedicate a book to a fool & that the first edition must be canceled.... Morgan had had five weeks to make up his mind.' Afterwards he told his mother in letters from Tunis that he had always thought Morgan '*a little fool*' and that his writing must invariably 'bring discomfort to fools, since it is agressive, witty, & unrelenting'. He declared that it was 'a relief not to have a cad's name on the first page' of his first play.

In spite of a more cautious second telegram from Firbank stating his unwillingness to be put to much expense, Richards took the matter up with the binders and found that after all it would be possible to substitute a cancel for the dedication leaf at a reasonable cost. He notified Peacock and Goddard to that effect on 13 November. Ten days later he wrote to Firbank in Tunis to say that copies of the book had been sent him there and that it would appear on the 26th, another of Firbank's lucky days. The next month Richards received a letter which Morgan had written from Madrid on 2 December to thank him and Firbank for 'being so obliging'.

Morgan's account of these events, written twenty years later, differs in details. After describing the 'style of the dedication' as 'that high flowing and beautiful prose of the French 18th Century', he went on,

> It had long been a standing joke that I should be called 'Cardinal Morgan' — it was much about this time that I myself had taken to considering becoming a Roman Catholic and I had been busying myself with ritual and Church practices. Unfortunately the dedication was brought to the notice of my family, precisely by

A. BOOKS AND PAMPHLETS

whom I shall never know, but I was sent post haste to Grant Richards to tell them that unless the book was published without the dedication my father would take steps against the author and publisher. Just about this time I was about to be posted as equerry to Lord Aberdeen, then Viceroy of Ireland, and for some obscure reason it was assumed that this dedication in the most faultless prose would be a deterrent to my gaining this exalted post, one which I may say I never acquired. The book was published without the dedication. I naturally had a bitter letter from the author and a sarcastic one from the publisher and found myself the victim of a good deal of adverse criticism on the part of the Firbank cult which had already started. Ronald did not speak to me for two years. (Copy of original letter belonging to Richard Buckle.)

No example of the book as first printed is available. On 1 December 1920 Richards asked Sevier to return his copy, which contained the dedication, and exchange it for one which did not. That he did so has not been established.

The memorandum of agreement for *The Princess Zoubaroff*, dated 7 June 1920, stipulated that the author pay the cost plus $33\frac{1}{3}$ per cent of producing an edition of 500 copies and that he receive the proceeds of sales less Richards's commission of 15 per cent; Firbank also agreed to pay for advertising. These costs came to a total of £112. 4s. 2d. A second memorandum dated 13 June provided for illustrations. For these and for the preparation of frontispiece and wrapper, Firbank paid £93. 5s. The cost of the cancel is unavailable.

G. P. Putnam's Sons asked to consider *The Princess Zoubaroff* for American publication, and Richards sent them a copy on 11 December 1920. Putnam's decided not to publish.

Firbank was eager to see his play on the stage, and in the late summer of 1921 he discussed the possibility at some length with Lillah McCarthy. She agreed to present the play in a twelve weeks' season of repertory. To finance the production, Lady Firbank, encouraged by her son, asked Sir Joseph Duveen to provide £1000. Nothing came of this scheme.

The Princess Zoubaroff was presented in early June 1951 at the Watergate Theatre with Faith Owen in the title-role. *The Times* reviewed the production on Saturday 9 June (p. 8). Brenda Dean Paul played the part of the Princess in a production of 1952 at the Irving Theatre, London. On 8 March and 8 April 1962, the BBC presented an adaptation of *The Princess Zoubaroff* by Archie Campbell on its Third Programme; Edith Evans played the title part. On 11 April 1975, the Tavistock Repertory Company presented the play at the Tower Theatre, Islington, with Valerie Testa as Zoubaroff. *The Times*'s review appeared on Saturday 12 April 1975.

A. BOOKS AND PAMPHLETS

A8   SANTAL   1921

a. First edition:

SANTAL | BY | RONALD FIRBANK | [*publisher's device*] | LONDON | GRANT RICHARDS LTD. | ST MARTIN'S STREET | 1921

Demy 8°. 9" × 5¾". 48 pp.

P. [1] half-title; p. [2] blank; p. [3] title; p. [4] imprint, 'PRINTED IN GREAT BRITAIN BY THE RIVERSIDE PRESS LIMITED | EDINBURGH'; p. [5] dedication, 'To | 'Ελένη.'; p. [6] blank; pp. 7-[42] text; pp. [43-8] integral catalogue of books 'BY THE SAME AUTHOR'.

Issued in rose stiff paper covers, 9¼" × 6". Lettered in dark blue on upper cover: SANTAL | BY | RONALD FIRBANK; along spine, upward: SANTAL BY RONALD FIRBANK; plate marked in Persian blue at top right corner of upper cover and bottom left corner of lower cover, a crescent moon 2" from tip to tip. Printed on white laid paper watermarked: WALDORF; white laid endpapers uniformly watermarked. Top edge rough trimmed; other edges deckle. Page sizes vary from 8⅝" × 5½" to 9" × 5¾".

Published 8 September 1921 at 7s. 6d.; 300 copies were printed. The British Library copy is dated 27 October 1921.

Both the composition and publication of *Santal* went smoothly. Firbank's first reference to it occurred in a letter to Lady Firbank from Algiers dated 1 October 1920. By the 7th he had planned his book. A letter of that date from Constantine, also directed to his mother, said,

> I expect to reach Tunis towards the end of November & with enough notes to make a story of — I want to rewrite Odette in an Arab setting — a child seeking Allah — I shall try & make the descriptions of scenery beautiful & keep the whole thing as simple as possible. I shall call the story '*Santal*,' which is the name of a perfume of the East.

He had already asked her to send him a copy of the Koran, in English. Visits that same month to Batna and Biskra enriched his experience, so that by 30 October he felt competent to start *Santal*. By 19 December the first part was complete. In January he added 'a few beautiful touches' as well as some 'useful things' got from excursions to Sfax, Gabes, and Kairouan (at Gabes he spent much of his time on a muezzin's balcony observing Tunisian village life). On 6 March 1921, writing from Tunis, Firbank told his mother he had finished *Santal* that morning. He was happy to have remained in Tunis long enough to do so, for he believed that he had thereby 'caught and fixed' some of the 'fascination of the East' in his book.

Having had *Santal* typed in Rome by a Russian princess, Firbank returned to England with it in late spring. Shortly after 3 June 1921

A. BOOKS AND PAMPHLETS

he reached an agreement with Richards whereby the author paid the cost plus $33\frac{1}{3}$ per cent of producing an edition of 300 copies. The actual production costs came to £40. 1s. of which Lady Firbank contributed £20 as a gift to her son. Firbank also agreed to pay for advertising and reviews; thus his total expenditures amounted to £90. 10s. 6d. In return he was to receive the proceeds of sales less a 15 per cent commission.

Impatient for the book's publication, Firbank urged that it come out in July. That was not possible, and it was scheduled for 8 September, a date Firbank chose as one of good omen. He received an early copy on 20 August and promptly wanted to add the title to the lower cover, but the manufacture of the book was too advanced for such a change.

The Helen of the dedication was Mrs Carewe, a sympathetic friend of many years. In the bleak days just after the war she had urged him to disregard his 'nervous apprehension about life' far enough to meet the Sitwells. Later she arranged Lord Berners's introduction to Firbank. Mrs Carewe suggested the Greek form of her name and wrote it so for Firbank's use.

b. First American edition (1955):

santal [*in large brown decorative letters*] | RONALD FIRBANK

Demy 8°. $8\frac{1}{2}''\times 5\frac{1}{2}''$. [vi], 58 pp.

Pp. [i–ii] blank; p. [iii] half-title; p. [iv] publisher's notice: 'BONACIO & SAUL | *with* GROVE PRESS'; p. [v] title; p. [vi] Library of Congress catalogue card number, imprint: '*Designed & printed by The Caliban Press* | *in The United States of America*', and reservation of rights; p. [1] fly-title; p. [2] blank; pp. 3–[56] text; pp. [57–8] blank. Chapter divisions, which occur on the lower fourth of pp. 3, 27, 33, 41, and 53, are marked by a numeral $\frac{7}{16}''$ in height; each of these is followed by only 5 lines of text. The pages are otherwise blank; pp. [26], [32], [40], and [52] are blank.

Issued in maroon cloth boards; blocked along spine, downward, in bright blue decorative letters: SANTAL. Printed on white laid paper; bright blue wove endpapers. Top and bottom edges rough trimmed; fore edge deckle. Oatmeal tan paper dust-jacket lettered in brown and black.

Published 9 March 1955 at $3; the publisher states that probably 500 copies were printed. The Library of Congress copy is dated 24 March 1955.

The text is that of the first edition (A8a).

A. BOOKS AND PAMPHLETS

A9   THE FLOWER BENEATH THE   1923
                      FOOT

a. First edition:

THE | FLOWER BENEATH | THE FOOT | BEING A RECORD OF THE EARLY LIFE OF | ST. LAURA DE NAZIANZI AND THE | TIMES IN WHICH SHE LIVED | [*black and white half-tone portrait by Wyndham Lewis*] | BY | RONALD FIRBANK | WITH A DECORATION BY C. R. W. NEVINSON |AND PORTRAITS BY AUGUSTUS JOHN | AND WYNDHAM LEWIS | LONDON | GRANT RICHARDS LTD. | 1923

Crown 8°. $7\frac{3}{8}''$ × $4\frac{7}{8}''$. 224 pp., conjugate frontispiece and title leaves, and 8-page catalogue of Firbank's books inserted.

Pp. [1-2] blank; p. [3] half-title; p. [4] imprint, 'PRINTED IN GREAT BRITAIN BY THE RIVERSIDE PRESS LIMITED | EDINBURGH'; frontispiece, black and white half-tone portrait by Augustus John (with protective tissue), and title on verso and recto respectively (reverse sides blank) of white linen-finish coated paper conjugate leaves tipped in between pp. [4] and [5]; p. [5] dedication, 'To | Madame Mathieu and | Mademoiselle Dora Garnier-Pagès'; p. [6] blank; p. [7] two epigraphs; p. [8] blank; pp. 9-224 text; 8-page catalogue, unpaginated, of books 'BY THE SAME AUTHOR'.

Issued in black cloth boards. Lettered in gilt on upper cover: THE FLOWER BENEATH THE FOOT; across spine: THE | FLOWER | BENEATH | THE FOOT | RONALD | FIRBANK | GRANT | RICHARDS. Printed on cream white wove paper; cream white calendered endpapers of lighter stock with 'decoration' by C. R. W. Nevinson, a bright blue and white line cut, on upper board paper. Top edge trimmed, stained green; other edges rough trimmed. Grey linen-finish coated paper dust-jacket lettered in dark grey and decorated with reproduction of Nevinson illustration.

Published 17 January 1923 at 7s. 6d.; 1,000 copies were printed. The British Library copy is dated 6 April 1923.

From start to finish the production of *The Flower Beneath the Foot* was slow and difficult. Firbank had hardly started writing *Santal* before he developed 'a scheme' for his next book. He wrote to his mother from Tunis on 9 November 1920 that he had 'a wonderful plan for a novel which ought to be a surprise for all the people who have disbelieved in me'. When he went to Palermo in March of the next year he was already 'busy making notes' for the book, but he had not decided yet 'where to settle in order to write it'. He thought seriously of New York or Vienna, but after travelling the usual route from Naples to Venice and then by Milan and Paris to London (he

A. BOOKS AND PAMPHLETS

arrived in late May), Firbank was still looking for a 'suitable place' in which to start his new novel. He decided on Versailles, and there in spite of the hot summer months and hordes of tourists, he made considerable progress. But at Montreux, where he went in November for a three months' stay, writing was well-nigh impossible. He suffered from a poorly heated chalet, and he complained bitterly about his neighbours: 'even when they are not chattering on the other side of the wall (they are four, with two servants, gardeners, dogs etc) you feel all the time they are *there* & it is impossible to write until they've gone'. As soon as the lease terminated at Montreux, Firbank moved on to Florence and then to a villa at Fiesole. He was still uneasy about his choice of a place to work. 'How different my book would have been had I gone to Vienna', he wrote to Lady Firbank on 25 February 1922, 'for of course one's surroundings tell. Probably it would have been more brilliant & flippant, but not as good as the steady work I hope to do here.' Undesirable servants and intrusions from his landlord hindered that steady work to a degree, but in a letter of 20 March he happily reported progress to his mother and described the book as 'quite in the style of Valmouth, vulgar cynical & "horrid," but of course beautiful here & there for those that can see'. At last on 23 May 1922 he wrote that he had finished *The Flower* the day before and that he thought it 'very *radiant*'.

He took it to Richards the next month, and on 30 June 1922 Firbank concluded the agreement for publication. In this he contracted to pay the cost plus $33\frac{1}{3}$ per cent of manufacturing 1,000 copies (only 502 to be bound immediately) and to receive the proceeds of sales less 15 per cent. Richards estimated the cost of manufacture at £115, of which £6 was allowed for printing a plain dust-jacket. The actual cost charged to Firbank's account, inclusive of binding 1,000 copies, advertising, and rent of standing type was £208. 17s. 5d. The agreement further stipulated that the book be produced uniform with Firbank's earlier cloth-bound books, but that the binding material be improved so as to resemble the cloth used for Charles Whibley's *Book of Scoundrels*.

Problems arose at once. The first was that of illustrations. Richards advised against the use of two portraits and urged Firbank to hold the John drawing for the next book; but Firbank persisted in printing both, though he admitted that the Lewis was 'wildly obscure' and that the portraits together were 'excessive'. Firbank provided them, but he left Lewis's copyright and fee to Richards, who also made all arrangements with Nevinson for the jacket design. Then, as usual, there was difficulty over language and punctuation. Richards wrote a long letter on the virtues of consistent punctuation, and he questioned the use of 'depreciated' for 'deprecated' (p. 13) and 'organicly' for 'organically' (p. [7]).

Furthermore, publication was postponed twice. Scheduled for October, the book was first withheld owing to Richards's fear of action for libel. A set of page proofs which establishes a state of the novel prior to publication contains unmistakable and libellous allusion

A. BOOKS AND PAMPHLETS

to Evan Morgan. These proofs differ from the published book in several ways. They lack dedication and frontispiece. The title-page of the proofs, p. [5], is printed on text paper; it is integral with p. 12 and thus a part of the first signature. The title lacks the drawing of Firbank by Wyndham Lewis and has, instead, a publisher's device. The title also lacks the legend below Firbank's name and Richards's address; the date 1922 is in Roman numerals. The imprint, uniform with that of the first edition (A9a), is on p. [6]. The first of the two epigraphs on p. [7] of the proofs retains Firbank's spelling 'organicly'. Page 224 lacks the dates '*July* 1921, *May* 1922' and the names of the three cities '*Versailles, Montreux, Florence*' which appear on p. 224 of the published book. The texts of the advertisements also differ from those published. The most significant difference between the published book and the set of proofs is the designation in the proofs (pp. 92-107) of the character Eddie Monteith of the published book as Heaven Organ. By that name was meant Evan Morgan. The name and the characterization were intended as retaliation for Morgan's refusal of the dedication of *The Princess Zoubaroff* (A7) and for his defection in friendship. The name is also a contemptuous allusion to the sexual relationship which had once existed between Morgan and Firbank. But in a letter of 23 September 1922, Grant Richards insisted on the danger of such usage, and Firbank changed his character's name from Heaven Organ to Eddie Monteith.

Even then, because *The Flower* made obvious reference to a number of prominent people, Firbank called it 'a most "dangerous" little book'. He identified many of the characters for his mother:

'Princess Elsie' = Princess Mary. 'Mrs Chilleywater' = Mrs Harold Nicolson. 'Eddy' = Evan Morgan — & of course 'King Geo' & 'Queen Glory' are the king & queen. The English Ambassadress is founded on Mrs Roscoe & Lady Nicolson.... The lady journalist must be 'Eve' of the Tatler or any other of the prattling busybodies that write for the magazines.

Firbank had agreed not only to change the name from Heaven Organ to Eddie Monteith but also to correct the spelling of 'organicly'. And Richards had agreed to use Augustus John's portrait of Firbank as the frontispiece and Wyndham Lewis's drawing on the title-page. The two men could not agree at once, however, on a new publication date. Richards wanted to publish in the latter half of November. But Firbank maintained that a book appearing in late November must be regarded as a Christmas item, and he refused to authorize release before January 1923. The matter was settled in that way; Firbank wrote to Van Vechten on 8 November 1922 that his book, 'timed for early New Year', would 'race the first white lilac'. His pre-publication copy was posted 10 January 1923.

Within a few months after the publication of *The Flower Beneath the Foot*, the relationship between Firbank and Richards was so impaired that it could never again be entirely mended. The breach apparently began with Firbank's dissatisfaction with the statement

A. BOOKS AND PAMPHLETS

of his account for the six months to the end of 1922. Actually no single incident could explain so complex a situation.

Undoubtedly one factor was Firbank's correspondence with Carl Van Vechten. Van Vechten began it in early 1922, and the exchange of letters developed a friendship which allowed Van Vechten to ask about Firbank's financial arrangements with Richards (cf. p. 32). Firbank's reply, written on 22 April 1923, said that in nine years he had 'never seen back *one* farthing piece' of the six or seven hundred pounds spent to produce his books. 'It seems', he wrote, 'that "the returns" from one book barely cover "the outgoings" of the next, — & so it goes on." Firbank apologized for discussing 'this sordid and unattractive side of authorship' and wondered whether he had been unfair to Richards, but the situation rankled none the less.

Much more important was Firbank's disappointment at the sales of his books and the feeling that Richards in every case could have done more to increase sales. In a letter from Rome in April 1921 he told his mother that he was 'furious' with Richards for 'neglecting to push' *The Princess Zoubaroff* (A7). 'He has simply collared my money & put the play on the shelf', Firbank wrote. As a result, he gave serious thought to taking *Santal* (A8a) elsewhere and decided not to only because he concluded it would 'be a *mistake* to leave Richards with a story so slight as Santal'; he feared that without Richards the book might be 'passed by unnoticed'. The number of letters between author and publisher on the matter of reviews, advertisements, where to place them, and their costs was enormous. Sometimes Lady Firbank wrote to Richards on her son's behalf; she suggested in March 1915 that a 'kind review [of *Vainglory* (A2a)] from Mr Robert Ross, for instance, would be such a stimulus'. She wrote again just before the appearance of *Caprice* (A5), and in May 1922 Lady Firbank inquired almost wistfully about her son's continued loss on his books. Richards was invariably gentle with her in his replies — that critics were slow to praise new kinds of work; that a man who put his individuality into his work, and he cited as examples T. Sturge Moore, Joseph Conrad, Samuel Butler, George Meredith, John Davidson, had little immediate success; or that Ronald made 'no concessions' — but with the son Richards was increasingly frank and often impatient. In August 1921 he wrote that if Firbank would look at *Santal*, he must agree that everything possible had been done to advertise his earlier works. When Firbank inquired in May 1923 about the sales of *The Flower*, Richards told him plainly that the London booksellers had not done well with his books and refused to credit the possibility that *The Flower* would 'turn the scale'. Sales of that title, especially in view of the edition of 1,000 instead of the usual 500, were most disappointing; only 456 had gone.

Firbank had expected large returns from *The Flower*. In December 1922, from Bordighera, he had asked to postpone payment of the amount still owed towards *The Flower* (£66) 'until Easter when the sales should recover the amount'. According to Firbank, Richards's reply was 'like a shark', but the bill was renewed. In May when he

A. BOOKS AND PAMPHLETS

inquired about sales, he fully believed there were several hundred pounds to his credit. This time he described Richards's answer as having the 'atmosphere of a dog with a stolen bone which its trying to hide'. Convinced now that he must put his 'writing on a different basis, & if necessary find a new publisher', Firbank declared to his mother that he intended to request an audit at once.

Then early in June 1923 Firbank received Richards's statement for the latter half of 1922. An accompanying letter explained that the cost of producing *The Flower* had been charged to the account, but none of the proceeds from 1923 sales of that or other novels had been credited, so that the author's account was 'practically' in balance. This explanation failed to satisfy Firbank. Writing from Bordighera on 7 June 1923 he told his mother about Richards, 'He has sent me a statement which kept me awake a whole night from indignation at his effrontery! ! . . . it appears he sold in the last year £225 of my books & that I still owe him 3/6!' On 18 June Firbank sent a carefully drafted letter to Richards questioning the entire statement:

> I fear I do not follow the statement you send me, for it is quite plain that in June 1922 there was a balance considerably over £100, in my favour, part of which sum went to cover the additional expenses of 'Santal' & the rest going towards the production of 'The Flower Beneth the Foot', necessitating an expenditure of a further £66, for which I sent you a cheque. So that the Author's sales from June 1922 to Dec 1922 are a seperate matter entirely, my cheque of £66 together with the credit due to me last June [£84] balancing matters. The sales from the latter half of last year, as I have them from Mr Wiggins (March 2nd) are —
> Inclinations 47
> Vainglory 71
> Odette 14
> Valmouth 103
> Princess Zoubaroff 42
> So that I cannot but be puzzled by your statement shewing the 'balance due to Publisher at the end of 1922 to be 3/6!'
> I find since 1914 I have spent not far short of £1000 on the production of my books & it is not unreasonable in 1923 to be expecting some return.
> My novels in New York are fetching big prices. In Knopf's list January 1923 [Blanche W. Knopf, 220 West 42nd Street, List 2], Valmouth published 7/6 is priced seven dollars (30/-) Odette 1/- (16/-) & meanwhile I have received nothing for my work over a span of soon ten years.

To this he had no reply, and on 25 June, back in London, he accused Richards of ignoring the letter. Firbank promptly received a memorandum dated 26 June; in it George Wiggins took up Firbank's complaints one by one.

Firbank was still not satisfied. He engaged W. B. Peat and Company to check Richards's accounts, and on 5 July 1923 that firm

A. BOOKS AND PAMPHLETS

obtained permission to examine the publisher's records. Peat and Company denied Richards's request for a copy of their report.

Meanwhile Firbank had placed the matter in the hands of the Society of Authors. No later than 2 August 1923 the Society began its attempts to collect whatever was due to Firbank from Richards. The letters which followed show considerable reluctance on Richards's part to come to a settlement. At last, however, on 9 May 1924 Richards sent a statement of Firbank's account, and on 31 May, after satisfying the secretary's objections to the statement, closed the account for 1923 with a cheque for £54. 0s. 2d. Further correspondence as half-yearly accounts fell due produced little additional income. After 31 May 1924, of the eight Firbank titles which Grant Richards had published, only *Odette* (A4) was in stock. Richards's statement showed 1,470 on hand. By 1929, 972 were still unsold, for in September of that year Duckworth collected the stock of *Odette*, 926 copies from the premises of the Society of Authors at 11 Gower Street and 46 from the Richards Press. Duckworth and the Society agreed to share equally in any proceeds realized from the sale of these copies.

b. First American edition (1924):

THE | FLOWER BENEATH | THE FOOT | BEING A RECORD OF THE EARLY LIFE OF | ST. LAURA DE NAZIANZI AND THE | TIMES IN WHICH SHE LIVED | BY | RONALD FIRBANK | [*black and white half-tone portrait*] | PORTRAIT BY WYNDHAM LEWIS | NEW YORK | BRENTANO'S | PUBLISHERS

Crown 8°. $7\frac{5}{16}'' \times 4\frac{7}{8}''$. x, 230 pp., and frontispiece.

P. [i] half-title; p. [ii] blank; frontispiece, reproduction of first edition's 'decoration' in bright orange and white line cut with legend in bright orange 'ILLUSTRATION BY C. R. W. NEVINSON' on white linen-finish coated paper (with protective tissue), tipped in facing p. [iii]; p. [iii] title; p. [iv] copyright notice, reservation of rights, and imprint, 'PRINTED IN THE UNITED STATES OF AMERICA'; pp. [v–vii] facsimile reproduction of Firbank's autograph signed preface within single-rule black frame; p. [viii] blank; p. [ix] dedication, '*To* | MADAME MATHIEU | AND | MADEMOISELLE DORA GARNIER-PAGÈS'; p. [x]; two epigraphs; p. [1] fly-title; p. [2] blank; pp. 3–229 text; p. [230] blank.

Issued in black cloth boards. Lettered in gilt on upper cover: THE FLOWER BENEATH THE FOOT; across spine: THE | FLOWER | BENEATH | THE FOOT | RONALD | FIRBANK | BRENTANO'S. First four leaves are cream white coated paper; otherwise printed on cream white laid paper; cream white wove endpapers of lighter stock.

A. BOOKS AND PAMPHLETS

Top edge trimmed, stained green; other edges rough trimmed. Grey linen-finish dust-jacket lettered in orange and decorated with reproduction of frontispiece.

Published October 1924 at $2; the number of copies printed cannot be ascertained. A letter which Stuart Rose wrote from New York on 3 October 1924 stated, 'derinden *The Flower Beneath the Foot* is scheduled for publication next week.' Announced in Camden, New Jersey *Courier*, 30 September 1924, and *New York Post*, 18 October 1924, as 'forthcoming'. Noted by *New York Post*, 1 November 1924, in 'Books on Our Table' and *Publishers' Weekly*, 1 November 1924. Brentano's named 20 October 1924 as publication date on its application for copyright. The Library of Congress copy is dated 7 November 1924.

The agreement for publication is dated 6 October 1924.

The text is a corrected version of the first edition. On 10 July 1924 Firbank posted to Brentano's approved proofs which, according to his own statement, were not used for the first edition. In an accompanying letter he listed two textual alterations: '*Pages* 22 & 84. "his Lankiness, Prince Olaf" might read "his naughtiness, Prince Olaf".' He also corrected one misprint: '*p.* 128. "But to Three I cling" should read, "Thee".'

After considerable success with *Prancing Nigger* (A10a), Brentano's had proposed to publish an American edition of Firbank's works commencing with *The Flower Beneath the Foot*. Albert and Charles Boni had also offered to bring out an American edition, but Firbank decided to continue with Brentano's. 'One publisher', he said, 'was better than gadding as Saint Theresa did.' Thus in a letter from Rome dated 17 May 1924 and addressed to Stuart Rose, Firbank agreed to write a preface for the American *Flower*. He declared that the preface offered an opportunity to remove the prejudice about his 'supposed depravity & lack of design'. In the same letter he suggested reproducing the Nevinson drawing as the frontispiece. The preface was sent off with the proofs on 10 July 1924.

A10   PRANCING NIGGER   1924

a. First edition:

PRANCING NIGGER | BY | RONALD FIRBANK | WITH AN INTRODUCTION BY | CARL VAN VECHTEN | [*orange, diamond shaped publisher's device in blind stamped diamond frame*] | NEW YORK | BRENTANO'S | PUBLISHERS

Crown 8°. $7\frac{3}{8}'' \times 4\frac{7}{8}''$. [2], xii, 126 pp., and frontispiece.
Printer's blank leaf, not reckoned in pagination; p. [i] half-title;

A. BOOKS AND PAMPHLETS

p. [ii] blank; frontispiece, half-tone in colour within single-rule black frame with legend 'Illustration by Robert E. Locher' on white coated paper (with protective tissue), tipped in facing p. [iii]; p. [iii] title; p. [iv] copyright notice, reservation of rights, and imprint, 'PRINTED IN THE UNITED STATES OF AMERICA'; pp. v–xi Preface, 'AN ICING FOR A CHOCOLATE ECLAIR' p. v and with 'Preface' as a running head pp. vi–xi, signed 'Carl Van Vechten' and dated *'New York, January 23, 1924'*; p. [xii] blank; p. [1] fly-title; p. [2] blank; pp. 3–126 text.

Issued in black cloth boards. Lettered in gilt on upper cover: PRANCING NIGGER; across spine: PRANCING | NIGGER | RONALD | FIRBANK | BRENTANO'S. Printed on cream white wove paper; cream white wove endpapers of lighter stock. Top edge trimmed, stained green; other edges rough trimmed. White linen-finish coated paper dust-jacket lettered in black and orange and decorated with a reproduction of the frontispiece within single-rule black frame.

Published March 1924 at $2; the number of copies printed cannot be ascertained. The first impression may have consisted of 300 copies; a letter from Carl Van Vechten to Firbank dated April [1924] stated: 'I think almost all — perhaps quite all — of the 300 copies of the first edition have been sold.' Noted by the *Boston Evening Transcript*, 15 March 1924; *Publishers' Weekly*, 22 March 1924. Brentano's named 11 March 1924 as publication date on its application for copyright. The Library of Congress copy is dated 18 March 1924.

When Van Vechten wrote in April about the sale of three hundred copies of *Prancing Nigger*, he added, 'The second edition is printing.' Van Vechten doubtless referred to a second printing issued that month. The second printing is uniform with the first except for p. [iv] to which is added, after reservation of rights, *'First Printing, March, 1924. Second Printing, April, 1924.'* In some copies of the second printing and possibly in all, an errata slip of coated paper, 5" × 5", is tipped in at the centre of the recto of the first free endpaper. Twenty-two errors are listed. A third printing was issued two years later. On p. [iv] is added, *'Third Printing, February, 1926.'* All errors listed on the errata sheet of the second printing except two are corrected in this printing.

Prancing Nigger was Firbank's first book-publication in America (cf. C8). He had hoped to publish there at least since August 1916, when he wrote from Torquay to Richards about the proofs of *Odette* (A4), 'Yesterday the wind bore off with them seawards. This must be a *favourable omen* for America!' But no American publisher had been willing to bring out his books. Inquiries from G. P. Putnam's Sons about *Caprice* (A5) and *The Princess Zoubaroff* (A7) came to nothing. Walter Peacock of Thomas Seltzer had asked to see a complete set of Firbank's works, and Grant Richards posted them on 16 July 1921. Richards wrote again and again to Seltzer and his English representative Douglas Goldring before receiving a refusal dated 10 April 1922. Although Firbank's novels were still under consideration

A. BOOKS AND PAMPHLETS

by Alfred Knopf in the spring of 1922, Richards concluded the demand was too small to justify an American publisher either in buying an edition or making separate publication. In a letter of 29 April 1922 he gave it as his opinion that no large sale of 'advanced modern work could be counted on in America' and that if *Valmouth* (A6a), as an example, were published there it would 'no doubt meet the same fate as "Jurgen" and with more reason'.

Early in 1922, however, Stuart Rose of Brentano's called Carl Van Vechten's attention to *Valmouth*. Almost at once Van Vechten prepared an article about Firbank, which appeared in *The Double Dealer* (III [April 1922], 185-7). He also wrote to Firbank stating his intention to make the novelist better known in America and asking for personal details. Firbank replied from Fiesole on 29 March 1922 with the information that he usually wrote with purple ink and that, though he was older, he admitted only to nineteen. Actually he had no idea who Carl Van Vechten was; but even after Richards told him that Van Vechten was a 'fairly well-known and very modern American critic', Firbank's letters maintained the same flippant tone for some time. Meanwhile, after much coaxing, he sent Van Vechten a chapter from *Prancing Nigger*, then named *Sorrow in Sunlight*, for publication in the Richmond, Virginia, quarterly *The Reviewer* (C8). This chapter apparently convinced Van Vechten that Firbank's new novel must be published in America.

Firbank had begun to plan the novel in July 1922. A letter to his mother written at that time from London said that his next would be 'a negro novel with a brilliant background of sunlight, sea, and as tropical' as he could make it. Thus he decided to return to Jamaica, and he asked Lady Firbank to arrange a reduced student fare for him on a ship of the Elder Dempster Lines. She could not do so; but in August he sailed from Liverpool in the RMS *Orcoma*, disembarking first at Cuba. And there, as he wrote from Santiago on 9 September, he ' "found" ' his book. 'Cuba', he declared in a letter from Kingston, Jamaica dated 19 September 1922, 'gave me all I needed for another novel.' On his return from the Caribbean in October, Firbank settled for a long stay in Italy, and from Bordighera on 17 June 1923 he sent a letter to his mother saying that he had finished his book that morning:

> It is too soon & I am too tired of it to judge it — But as a bit of colour & atmosphere it is the best of all my others & some of the figures negroes & Spanish South Americans are as wonderful as their setting! It is an amazing affair altogether & some no doubt will be horrified by it while others will be carried away by its vivid unusualness & the crude touches left purposely unshaded.

As he told Van Vechten two days later, the new novel was then called 'Drama in Sunlight'.

His attitude toward Richards had deteriorated to such an extent — Richards was still largely unaware of the fact — that publication through him was impossible. According to Richards, Firbank offered

A. BOOKS AND PAMPHLETS

the book to C. S. Evans of Heinemann's, describing it as 'purposely a little "primitive," rather like a Gauguin in painting — extremely gay' (*Author Hunting*, London, 1960, p. 205). Evans was not interested. Then, as his letter to Lady Firbank written from Seville on 23 August stated, Firbank asked Elkin Mathews for an estimate on the cost of producing the new novel. But towards the end of the next month Firbank had a letter from Van Vechten dated 19 September 1923 suggesting publication in America; he and Stuart Rose had arranged for Brentano's to consider the book. Firbank promptly recovered his typescript from Elkin Mathews, and on 1 October sent it to New York. By 17 November he had heard that Brentano's planned to publish with the title 'Prancing Nigger'. Van Vechten had changed the title, and Firbank readily agreed; he found the new name 'delicious'. On 10 February he wrote to add a dedication '*For Roxanne*', but the book had already gone to press, even though the author's corrected copy had not yet reached New York.

He acknowledged a cheque from Rose on 13 July, 'I cannot tell you how delighted it makes me to receive this reward for my work — the first indeed after so long!' In October, when he had just received $695 from Brentano's, Firbank wrote to his sister, Heather, that now he could 'hope at last the ball' was 'set rolling'. Although this publication obviously marked a turn in Firbank's literary fortunes, his pleasure in it was not unadulterated. The many typographical errors in *Prancing Nigger* damped his enthusiasm; because of these he distributed almost no copies as gifts. Furthermore, there was a break in the 'lonely & isolated' existence which he had achieved by 'slow stages'. After Philip Moeller, armed with an introduction from Van Vechten and an account of American admiration, visited him in Rome in the early summer of 1924, Firbank told Heather, 'I feel alarmed . . . by these new friends that my books are bringing me. I feel often far too tired & their sympathy comes too late to make a *personal* success of my literary one!'

Several dramatic versions of *Prancing Nigger* have been made, but none has been presented in the theatre. In October 1924 Stuart Rose and Thurston Macauley, who was connected with the Cherry Lane Theatre of New York, asked Firbank's permission to dramatize the novel. They prepared a comedy adaptation in ten scenes with the title 'A Jazz Fantasy'. Their plans included a special musical score composed by George Gershwin and a mobile stage-set designed by Mordecai Gorelik. Philip Moeller and William Brady both considered the piece, but the cost of staging and the financial risk of so avant-garde a comedy were too great.

On 29 May 1931 Brentano's signed an agreement granting dramatic rights to Albert Johnston and Elizabeth England. These lapsed, and Miss England renewed them in a contract signed by her, Coward-McCann, and Thomas J. Firbank. The contract, dated August 1935, became effective on 24 June 1936. Apparently Miss England was working with the Century Play Company in a plan to turn *Prancing Nigger* into an operetta. Her version may have been the one for which

A. BOOKS AND PAMPHLETS

John La Touche wrote the lyrics and Vernon Duke was asked to compose the music.

By an agreement with Coward-McCann dated 15 February 1938, Dan Totheroh held dramatic rights for a time. In the previous year he had written an adaptation of Firbank's book intended as a musical for Broadway, and James Shelton had composed a tentative score. Totheroh showed his script to Charles B. Cochran and later to Moss Hart. Both liked the script, but each in turn thought its subject-matter made production too hazardous.

In the early 'thirties — the exact date is unknown — Metro-Goldwyn-Mayer proposed to film another musical comedy version. The scenario was prepared and MGM announced its plans. The name *Prancing Nigger* roused an outcry in the American negro press, and Nancy Cunard wrote a defence of Firbank and his use of the name for the Associated Negro Press under the date-line 'Paris, 18 November'. No year for this article can be determined, and Miss Cunard could not recall it. The motion picture was not made.

b. First English edition (1924):

SORROW IN SUNLIGHT | BY | RONALD FIRBANK | [*red diamond-shaped publisher's device*] | LONDON | BRENTANO'S LTD. | PUBLISHERS

Crown 8°. $7\frac{1}{2}'' \times 5''$. 128 pp.

P. [1] half-title; p. [2] blank; p. [3] title; p. [4] limitation notice, 'One Thousand Copies of | this Edition have been | printed, of which this is | No. [*number written in black ink*]', pp. 5-126 text; p. [127] imprint, 'PRINTED IN GREAT BRITAIN | BY UNWIN BROTHERS, LIMITED | PRINTERS, LONDON AND WOKING'; p. [128] blank.

Issued in black cloth boards. Lettered in gilt within single-rule frame in blind on upper cover: SORROW IN SUNLIGHT; across spine: SORROW | IN | SUNLIGHT | RONALD | FIRBANK | BRENTANO'S LTD. Printed on cream white laid paper; cream white calendered endpapers with illustration by C. R. W. Nevinson produced in black and white line. Top edge trimmed, stained green; fore edge untrimmed; bottom edge rough trimmed. White coated paper dust-jacket lettered in red and mauve and decorated with reproduction of *Prancing Nigger*'s frontispiece (A10a) within single-rule frame.

Published November 1924 at 7s. 6d.; 1,000 copies were printed. Noted by *The Morning Post*, 22 November 1924, in 'To-Day's Books'; *The Times*, 18 December 1924; *New Statesman*, 20 December 1924. The British Library copy is dated 6 November 1924.

Without being more specific both Muir ('Bibliography', p. 7) and the *English Catalogue* list the publication date as 1925.

A. BOOKS AND PAMPHLETS

The text is that of the first edition (A10a) with corrections in accordance with the errata sheet of the second printing.

By 27 June 1924 Firbank had reached an agreement with Brentano's, London, for a limited edition of *Prancing Nigger* under an earlier title *Sorrow in Sunlight*. Shortly after 20 August he received proof. At about that time he supplied the sketch used to decorate the endpapers, though he had hoped it might be reproduced for the dust-jacket. After the book appeared, Firbank declared it had come out in a 'furtive way', that Brentano's 'gauche mishandling' left people still asking when it was to be published.

In October 1929 Brentano's wanted to remainder 200 copies. The Society of Authors protested on the grounds that the memorandum of agreement made no provision for remaindering, and the matter was dropped.

c. New Readers Library edition (1931):

PRANCING NIGGER | by | RONALD FIRBANK | DUCKWORTH | 3 HENRIETTA STREET | LONDON, W.C.2

Foolscap 8°. $6\frac{3}{4}''$ × $4\frac{1}{2}''$. 128 pp. and 16-page publisher's catalogue inserted.

P. [1] half-title; p. [2] list of 'SOME VOLUMES IN | THE NEW READERS LIBRARY'; p. [3] title; p. [4] note on title 'Prancing Nigger', publication notice, and imprint, 'Made *and* Printed *in* Great Britain | *By* The Camelot Press Ltd. | London *and* Southampton'; pp. 5–126 text; p. [127] list of 'THE WORKS OF | RONALD FIRBANK' in the Rainbow edition (A12c); p. [128] blank; 16-page publisher's catalogue, undated, with title 'THE NEW READERS' LIBRARY', and note on p. [1], catalogue items on pp. 2–15, and on p. [16] imprint, '*Printed at the* BURLEIGH PRESS, *Lewin's Mead*, Bristol'.

Issued in bright blue cloth boards. Lettered in gilt across spine: PRANCING | NIGGER | RONALD | FIRBANK | DUCKWORTH with triple rule in gilt at head and tail. No dust-jacket available.

Published 7 May 1931 at 3*s.* 6*d.*; 1,500 copies were printed.

The text is that of *The Works* (A12a).

A11   CONCERNING THE ECCENTRICITIES   1926
OF CARDINAL PIRELLI

First edition:

CONCERNING THE | ECCENTRICITIES OF | CARDINAL PIRELLI | BY | RONALD FIRBANK | [*publisher's device*]

A. BOOKS AND PAMPHLETS

| LONDON | GRANT RICHARDS LTD. | ST MARTIN'S STREET | MDCCCCXXVI

Crown 8°. $7\frac{5}{16}''\times 4\frac{7}{8}''$. 152 pp. and frontispiece.

P. [1] blank; p. [2] list of '*BOOKS BY | RONALD FIRBANK*'; p. [3] half-title; p. [4] blank; frontispiece, portrait by Augustus John within five-rule frame produced in black and white half-tone on white linen-finish coated paper (with protective tissue), tipped in facing p. [5]; p. [5] title; p. [6] imprint, 'Printed in Great Britain | by The Riverside Press Limited | Edinburgh'; pp. 7-150 text; pp. [151-2] blank.

Issued in black cloth boards. Lettered in gilt on upper cover: CONCERNING THE ECCENTRICITIES | OF CARDINAL PIRELLI; across spine: CONCERNING | THE | ECCENTRICITIES | OF | CARDINAL | PIRELLI | RONALD | FIRBANK | GRANT | RICHARDS. Printed on cream white laid paper, cream white wove endpapers of lighter stock. Top edge trimmed, stained green; other edges rough trimmed. White linen-finish paper dust-jacket lettered in black and decorated with portrait by Charles Shannon produced in half-tone in colour within five-rule frame; the date 1925 on the dust-jacket has been changed to 1926 with black ink.

Published 29 June 1926 at 6*s.*; 1,000 copies were printed. The British Library copy is dated 17 June 1926. Grant Richards posted two copies to C. J. Herold of Brentano's, New York, on 6 July 1926 for copyright purposes. On 26 August 1926 Brentano's took out *ad interim* copyright.

All copies of the first edition contain a cancel title-leaf. Repeated delays in publication made necessary a change of date on the title. These delays account too for the alteration of the date on the dust-jacket.

Indeed, publication did not come until almost three years after the author first referred to *Cardinal Pirelli. En route* to Spain, on 12 August 1923 Firbank wrote to his mother from Paris that he hoped to return by September with enough notes for a book. Later that month, from Seville, he sent Van Vechten a description of Archbishop Ilundain y Esteban's palace and added, 'Needless to say I have not seen the great man, nor shall I ever, but he has suggested to my fancy a really amusing book.' On 1 December he wrote again, this time from Rome, saying he had started his Spanish novel and giving its name. In several letters after that he reported his progress until on 16 December 1924, in a letter to Stuart Rose, Firbank said that his book was finished except for the last chapter. 'Enfantments of Cardinals', he wrote, 'are slower than Niggers.' But at last, on 16 February 1925, he told Rose the book was finished, and he proposed to send it from London as soon as it was typed. Brentano's decided against publication on 'religious and moral grounds'. The firm feared that the 'outspokenness of the book regarding the life of the Cardinal and particularly church matters' would alienate its bookstore clientele.

A. BOOKS AND PAMPHLETS

Firbank then returned to Grant Richards. On 27 May 1925 the typescript along with a gift of the American edition of *The Flower Beneath the Foot* (A9b) was sent to Richards. Two days later Firbank and Richards entered into an agreement which stipulated that Firbank pay the cost of producing an edition of 1,000 copies plus 25 per cent and receive the proceeds of sales less 15 per cent. Block-making and special colour-printing for frontispiece and jacket were considered separately. Firbank wanted William Rothenstein to design both, but Rothenstein declared the work was not for anyone who had 'attained his ripe years'. Thus Firbank supplied a John portrait which he already had for the frontispiece and engaged Nevinson to design the jacket. Total costs including advertising amounted to £155. 8s.

Publication was intended for 1925, probably in October, for on 1 November Firbank wrote from Cairo to ask whether his three copies of *The Cardinal* had been sent him. But Richards's mounting financial difficulties had delayed the book. Labour unrest – packers, porters and binders were 'out' that month – prevented its appearance in November. December Firbank thought disadvantageous for sales, and in any case Richards's bankruptcy complicated the situation. Firbank, writing from Cairo on 17 December 1925, told Van Vechten, 'The Cardinal is being held up by Richards, who is I hear being made a bankrupt. Fortunately I am producing the book in England myself, so that its debut may be looked for directly G. R. can snatch a calm hour from the Bailiffs.' The book had to be postponed until 1926. Then, although Firbank sent both appeals and threats to the publisher, Richards allowed production to lag until it was made impossible by the General Strike, which began on 3 May 1926. When *Cardinal Pirelli* finally appeared, Firbank had been dead almost six weeks.

Although Richards had disposed of all copies by 18 August, the amount due to Firbank's estate was not paid for some months. Richards told Herold of Brentano's on that date that he had not the 'slightest idea' who Firbank's executors were. 'It is now several weeks since he died', Richards wrote, 'but no one has cropped up to show any interest in his affairs.'

In August 1925 a large paper edition limited to 250 signed copies was under consideration. Richards wrote to Firbank on 5 August that a bookseller had suggested such an edition. Firbank agreed to it on condition that the booksellers be reponsible for the edition to sell at £2. 2s. per copy and that he receive ten copies and £50 from sales. Richards explained that booksellers did not customarily underwrite editions, that his own firm must be responsible. Eventually the difficulties of producing the ordinary edition precluded a limited one, particularly in view of Firbank's demands.

A. BOOKS AND PAMPHLETS

A12   THE WORKS OF RONALD FIRBANK   1928

a. First collected edition limited, English issue:

Volume I:

THE WORKS OF | RONALD FIRBANK | VOL. I | INTRODUCTION| By ARTHUR WALEY | BIOGRAPHICAL MEMOIR | By OSBERT SITWELL | VAINGLORY | DUCKWORTH : LONDON | BRENTANO'S : NEW YORK | 1929

Demy 8°. $8\frac{3}{4}''$ X $5\frac{11}{16}''$. [2], x, 236 pp. and frontispiece.

Printer's blank leaf, not reckoned in pagination, conjugate with leaf numbered pp. [i] and [ii] and together pasted in; p. [i] series half-title; p. [ii] blank; p. [iii] limitation notice, 'Of this edition of the Works of Ronald Firbank in | five volumes there have been printed, on Abbey Mills | paper, by The Westminster Press, two hundred and | thirty-five copies, of which two hundred only are for | sale throughout the world. | No [*number written in black ink*]'; p. [iv] blank; frontispiece, portrait by Augustus John produced in black and white half-tone on white linen-finish coated paper (with protective tissue), tipped in facing p. [v]; p. [v] title; p. [vi] imprint, 'Printed in Great Britain at | The Westminster Press | 411a Harrow Road | London W. 9'; p. vii publication note on all titles and note on Firbank portraits in each volume of this series; p. viii blank; p. ix Contents of Vol. I; p. x blank; pp. 1-11 Introduction, with 'INTRODUCTION' as a running head pp. 2-11, signed 'ARTHUR WALEY'; pp. 12-34 Biographical Memoir, with 'BIOGRAPHICAL MEMOIR' as a running head pp. 13-34, signed 'OSBERT SITWELL'; p. [35] fly-title; p. [36] blank; pp. 37-[234] text; p. [235] blank; p. [236] colophon.

Volume II:

THE WORKS OF | RONALD FIRBANK | VOL. II | ODETTE | INCLINATIONS | CAPRICE | DUCKWORTH: LONDON | BRENTANO'S : NEW YORK | 1929

Demy 8°. $8\frac{11}{16}''$ X $5\frac{11}{16}''$. viii, 248 pp. and frontispiece.

Pp. [i-ii] blank; p. [iii] series half-title; p. [iv] blank; frontispiece, portrait by Wyndham Lewis produced in black and white half-tone on white linen-finish coated paper (with protective tissue), tipped in facing p. [v]; p. [v] title; p. [v] imprint, 'Printed in Great Britain at | The Westminster Press | 411a Harrow Road | London W. 9'; p. [vii] Contents of Vol. II; p. [viii] blank; p. [1]-[248] text.

A. BOOKS AND PAMPHLETS

Volume III:

THE WORKS OF | RONALD FIRBANK | VOL. III | VALMOUTH | THE PRINCESS ZOUBAROFF | DUCK- WORTH : LONDON | BRENTANO'S : NEW YORK | 1929

Demy 8°. $8\frac{11}{16}'' \times 5\frac{11}{16}''$. viii, 212 pp. and frontispiece.

Pp. [i–ii] blank; p. [iii] series half-title; p. [iv] blank; frontispiece, a portrait by Augustus John within five-rule border produced in black and white half-tone on white linen-finish coated paper (with protective tissue), tipped in facing p. [v]; p. [v] title, p. [vi] imprint, 'Printed in Great Britain at | The Westminster Press | 411a Harrow Road | London W. 9'; p. [vii] contents of Vol. III; p. [viii] blank; pp. [1]–[212] text.

Volume IV:

THE WORKS OF | RONALD FIRBANK | VOL. IV | SAN- TAL | THE FLOWER BENEATH | THE FOOT | DUCK- WORTH : LONDON | BRENTANO'S : NEW YORK | 1929

Demy 8°. $8\frac{11}{16}'' \times 5\frac{11}{16}''$. viii, 168 pp. and frontispiece.

Pp. [i–ii] blank; p. [iii] series half-title; p. [iv] blank; frontispiece, portrait by Charles Shannon within five-rule border produced in half-tone in colour on white linen-finish coated paper (with protective tissue), tipped in facing p. [v]; p. [v] title; p. [vi] imprint, 'Printed in Great Britain at | The Westminster Press | 411a Harrow Road | London W. 9'; p. [vii] Contents of Vol. IV; p. [viii] blank; pp. [1]–[168] text.

Volume V:

THE WORKS OF | RONALD FIRBANK | VOL. V | PRANCING NIGGER | CONCERNING | THE ECCENTRI- CITIES OF | CARDINAL PIRELLI | DUCKWORTH : LONDON | BRENTANO'S : NEW YORK : | 1929

Demy 8°. $8\frac{11}{16}'' \times 5\frac{11}{16}''$. viii, 152 pp. and frontispiece.

Pp. [i–ii] blank; p. [iii] series half-title; p. [iv] blank; frontispiece, portrait by Augustus John produced in black and white half-tone on white linen-finish coated paper (with protective tissue), tipped in facing p. [v]; p. [v] title; p. [vi] imprint, 'Printed in Great Britain at | The Westminster Press | 411a Harrow Road | London W. 9'; p. [vii]

A. BOOKS AND PAMPHLETS

Contents of Vol. V; p. [viii] blank; pp. [1]-[152] text with a note on the title 'Prancing Nigger', p. [3].

The five volumes issued uniformly in yellow buckram boards. Lettered in gilt across spine: THE WORKS | OF | RONALD | FIRBANK | [*volume number*]. Printed on cream white laid paper watermarked with a crown and 'Abbey Mills | Greenfield'; cream white laid endpapers watermarked uniformly. Top edges trimmed, stained green; other edges rough trimmed. Grey laid paper dust-jacket watermarked uniformly and lettered in black on spine.

The five volumes, all dated 1929, were published simultaneously on 10 December 1928. Of 240 sets printed, Duckworth offered 125 for sale at £5. 5s. the set. The British Library copy is dated 10 December 1928.

All the novels in these volumes had previously been published. Each novel is preceded by a fly-title and includes whatever dedication, divisional fly-title, epigraph, etc. may have appeared in the first edition with the added note on the title of *Prancing Nigger* as stated above (Vol. V, p. [3]). Although the publisher made minor textual revisions throughout, texts are those of the first editions except for *Odette*, which follows the text of the first separate illustrated edition, 1916 (A4). Two versions of Chapter IV, Part II, of *Inclinations* are printed consecutively (Vol. II, pp. 129-41). The second version is published for the first time. Firbank had been dissatisfied with *Inclinations* from the time he hurried to complete it in January 1916 (cf. p. 11). When he anticipated an American edition as proposed by Brentano's, New York, in March 1925, he began revision of this 'dinner party' chapter. The text of *Prancing Nigger* is corrected in accordance with the errata sheet of the second printing (A10a).

One of Ronald Firbank's last acts before his death was to ensure an edition of his collected works. It was a project dear to his heart. His hope — and expectation — that Brentano's would bring out such an edition was dashed by several things: Brentano's disinterest in an American issue of *Caprice* (A5; cf. pp. 15-16) in spite of a new preface, their outright rejection of *Cardinal Pirelli* (A11; cf. p. 36), and reluctance on the part of the London branch to make a definite commitment. Negotiations with Guy Chapman in the summer of 1925 for an edition underwritten by Firbank were not concluded satisfactorily. Then in April 1926, his awareness of his failing health sharpened by a cold caught during a stay in Cairo, Firbank made arrangements which assured a collected edition. By a deed of trust dated 23 April 1926 he empowered the Society of Authors to apply £1,000, which he paid to the Society, and interest thereon towards publication of a new edition of his works 'in the event of the death of the author within five years' from the date of the agreement. The deed provided for investment of the £1,000 in British Government securities.

The Society acted on this matter two years after Firbank's death. On 7 June 1928 the Committee of Management of the Society accepted Duckworth's proposal for a limited edition. The Committee

A. BOOKS AND PAMPHLETS

signed an agreement with Duckworth dated 14 September. By this agreement the Society advanced Duckworth £500 to produce 235 copies of a five-volume set, 35 being for review purposes. This sum, paid when the edition went to press, was credited to the Society in royalties, and eventually these repaid the entire £500. A commission of £100 was the publisher's sole remuneration.

In May 1934 a sixth volume, the limited edition (60 copies) of *The Artificial Princess* (A13b), was added to *The Works* by agreement between Duckworth and the Centaur Press. Sir Coleridge Kennard's introduction to *The Artificial Princess* (p. x) states that fact and the lettering on the dust-jacket reads, 'THE COLLECTED WORKS OF RONALD FIRBANK VOL. VI'. Copies are bound uniform with the five volumes of *The Works* and the stocks of the dust-jackets are identical. Otherwise this sixth volume differs in several respects: the preliminaries, the presence of illustrations, the stock on which it is printed, the text and position of the lettering on the spine, and the position of the lettering on the dust-jacket.

b. First collected edition limited, American issue (1929)

Brentano's imported bound copies of 110 sets uniform with the English issue. Of these, 100 were for sale in America at $30 the set. No release date can be determined. Reviewed by *New York Herald Tribune Books*, 5 May 1929. The set was not noted by *Publishers' Weekly*. No copyright application is recorded; no Library of Congress deposit was made.

The Committee of Management of the Society of Authors accepted Brentano's offer of publication on 3 July 1928. The exact arrangements with Brentano's have not been ascertained except for the fact that the sale in America was specifically limited to 100 sets.

Copies of the sixth volume as added to the English issue were not imported for sale in America.

c. Rainbow edition (1929-30):

The Rainbow edition consists of eight volumes published by Duckworth over a period of several months. The texts of all eight were printed from the same setting as *The Works* (A12a); appropriate preliminaries were added. Duckworth named the edition 'Rainbow' because of its variegated bindings and dust-jackets.

Volume I. *Prancing Nigger:*
PRANCING NIGGER | by | RONALD FIRBANK | DUCKWORTH | 3 HENRIETTA STREET | LONDON

A. BOOKS AND PAMPHLETS

Demy 8°. $8\frac{3}{16}''\times 5\frac{7}{16}''$. 80 pp.

Pp. [1-2] blank; p. [3] half-title; p. [4] list of works 'By Ronald Firbank' and notice, 'Other works in preparation'; p. [5] title; p. [6] note on the title 'Prancing Nigger' and publication note; pp. [7]-77 text; p. [78] colophon; pp. [79-80] blank.

Issued in orange cloth boards. Lettered in gilt along upper $2\frac{1}{4}''$ of spine, upward: PRANCING NIGGER. Printed on cream white laid paper; cream white wove endpapers. All edges trimmed. No dust-jacket available.

Published 7 February 1929 at 3s. 6d.; 1,500 copies were printed. The British Library copy is dated 18 June 1929.

P. [6] containing the note on the title with publication note added is reimposed.

The subsequent seven volumes are uniformly demy 8°. ($8\frac{3}{16}''\times 5\frac{7}{16}''$). In these seven volumes all half-titles occur on p. [1] and titles, on p. [3]. None contains a note on its title, though all have publication notes. All have imprint, 'Printed in Great Britain at the Westminster Press | 411a Harrow Road, London W. 9'; this is on p. [4] of each volume except *Caprice*, in which the imprint is on p. [96]. Only two, *Valmouth* and *The Princess Zoubaroff*, have the colophon. 1,500 copies of each title were printed; all sold at 3s. 6d. They were issued as follows:

    2 May 1929:   *Valmouth.* 128 pp.
                                 Green cloth boards; coral dust-jacket.
                                 British Library copy dated 18 June 1929.

    15 May 1929:   *The Flower Beneath the Foot.* 136 pp.
                                 Bright blue cloth boards; crimson dust-jacket.
                                 British Library copy dated 18 June 1929.

    5 July 1929:   *Concerning the Eccentricities of Cardinal Pirelli.* 80 pp.
                                 Purple cloth boards; bright blue dust-jacket.
                                 British Library copy dated 28 June 1929.

    5 September 1929:   *Caprice.* 96 pp.
                                 Yellow cloth boards; orchid dust-jacket.
                                 British Library copy dated 5 September 1929.

    5 September 1929:   *Inclinations.* 136 pp.
                                 Red cloth boards; orange dust-jacket.
                                 British Library copy dated 5 September 1929.

    9 January 1930:   *Vainglory.* 204 pp.
                                 Purple cloth boards; red dust-jacket.
                                 British Library copy dated 13 January 1930.

A. BOOKS AND PAMPHLETS

16 January 1930:   *The Princess Zoubaroff.* 96 pp.
Burnt-orange cloth boards; bright blue dust-jacket.
British Library copy dated 13 January 1930.

At its 6 November 1928 meeting the Committee of Management of the Society of Authors approved production of this inexpensive edition by Duckworth, who agreed to bear all costs and to pay 10 per cent to the Society, subject to settlement of any claim by Brentano's. In February 1940 Duckworth reissued the eight 'Rainbow' titles with a ninth, *The Artificial Princess*, added. The publisher's office states, 'We know definitely that *Prancing Nigger, The Flower Beneath the Foot*, and *Cardinal Pirelli* were reprinted by photography — 1000 of each at 4s. . . . There was a reprint of *Valmouth* of some kind, but we cannot find out how many. The other titles were merely brought up to 4s. sale price.' Apparently a considerable number of the 1929-30 impression of *Caprice, Inclinations, The Princess Zoubaroff*, and *Vainglory* — perhaps as many as 1,000, though the exact number cannot be determined — remained in the publisher's stock. A smaller number of copies of *Valmouth* was on hand; thus *Valmouth* was reprinted only to the extent needed to make its stock adequate. *The Artificial Princess* is a re-impression by photography of the first edition (A13a). Variegated bindings were retained. Dust-jackets of wove paper lettered in black and announcing the 'Rainbow' titles as 'now again available' were added; the only two examples inspected were both orange in colour.

d. Omnibus edition, English issue (1949-50):

The Omnibus edition, so designated by Duckworth, consists of the two volumes *Five Novels* and *Three Novels* published almost a year apart. The text of seven of the eight novels are re-impressions by photolithography of the texts of the Rainbow edition (A12c). The text of the eighth, *The Artificial Princess*, was reset for inclusion in *Five Novels*. The introductions of both volumes were printed from an original typesetting.

Volume I. *Five Novels:*
Ronald Firbank | [*swelled, beaded rule*] | FIVE NOVELS | VALMOUTH | THE FLOWER BENEATH THE FOOT | PRANCING NIGGER | CONCERNING THE ECCENTRICITIES | OF CARDINAL PIRELLI | THE ARTIFICIAL PRINCESS | *With an introduction by* | OSBERT SITWELL

A. BOOKS AND PAMPHLETS

| [*publisher's device*] | [*swelled, beaded rule*] | Gerald Duckworth & Co. Ltd. | 3 Henrietta St., LONDON, W.C.2
Demy 8°. $8\frac{3}{8}'' \times 5\frac{3}{8}''$. xxxii, 476 pp.

P. [i] half-title; p. [ii] frontispiece, portrait reproduced in black and white half-tone with legend, 'RONALD FIRBANK | (*from a drawing by* AUGUSTUS JOHN, R.A.)'; p. [iii] title; p. [iv] publication notice, reservation of rights, and imprint, 'Printed *in Great Britain by* | *Phototype Limited, London*'; p. [v] Contents; p. [vi] blank; pp. vii-xxxi Introduction, with 'INTRODUCTION' as a running head pp. viii-xxxi, signed 'OSBERT SITWELL'; p. [xxxii] blank; p. [1] fly-title; p. [2] blank; pp. 3-[123] text; p. [124] blank; p. [125] fly-title and dedication; p. [126] epigraph; pp. 127-256 text; p. [257] fly-title; p. [258] blank; pp. 259-329 text; p. [330] blank; p. [331] fly-title; p. [332] blank; pp. 333-406 text; p. 407 fly-title; p. [408] blank; p. [409] Contents; p. [410] blank; pp. 411-[72] text and at foot of page imprint, '*Printed in Great Britain by* | *Billing and Sons Ltd., Guildford and Esher*'; pp. [473-6] blank.

Issued in dark green cloth boards. Script blocked in gold foil across spine: Five | novels | by | Ronald | Firbank | Duckworth. Printed on white wove paper; white wove endpapers. All edges trimmed; top edge stained green. No dust-jacket available.

Published December 1949 at 18*s.*; 7,350 copies were printed of which 2,350 were bound and 5,000 exported in sheets for American issue. Noted by *The Bookseller*, 3 December 1949; *Manchester Guardian*, 9 December 1949; *Times Literary Supplement*, 16 December 1949. The British Library copy is dated 29 November 1949.

Two subsequent impressions were issued. The first, released in April 1950, consisted of 5,000 copies, of which 2,000 were bound and offered for sale at 18*s.* and 3,000 were exported in sheets to America. The second, issued in October 1951, consisted of 2,000 copies of which 1,500 were offered for sale at 21*s.* and 500 exported in sheets. Both impressions were uniform with the 1949 impression with these exceptions: the legend p. [ii] lacks parentheses in the 1951 impression; appropriate revisions of the publication notice p. [iv]; the imprint p. [472] in the 1950 impression reads, '*Printed in Great Britain by* | *Phototype Limited, London*'; the 1951 impression lacks imprint p. [472]; both lack pp. [473-6]. The 1951 impression was issued in yellow cloth boards with script blocked in gold foil on a dark green background across the spine.

Volume II. *Three Novels:*
Ronald Firbank | [*swelled, beaded rule*] | THREE NOVELS | VAINGLORY | INCLINATIONS | CAPRICE | *With an introduction by* | ERNEST JONES | [*publisher's device*] |

A. BOOKS AND PAMPHLETS

[*swelled, beaded rule*] | Gerald Duckworth & Co. Ltd. | 3 Henrietta St., London, W.C.2

Demy 8°. $8\frac{7}{16}"\times 5\frac{1}{2}"$. xx, 428 pp.

P. [i] half-title; p. [ii] frontispiece, portrait reproduced in black and white half-tone within triple-rule frame with legend, 'RONALD FIRBANK | from a pastel by Charles Shannon, R. A.'; p. [iii] title; p. [iv] publication notice, reservation of rights, and imprint, '*Printed in Great Britain by | Jas. Truscott & Son*, Ltd., *London and Tonbridge*.'; p. [v] Contents; p. [vi] blank; pp. vii–xx Introduction, with 'INTRODUCTION' as a running head pp. viii–xx, signed 'ERNEST JONES'; p. [1] fly-title; p. [2] blank; pp. 3–[200] text; p. [201] fly-title and division notice; p. [202] epigraph; pp. 203–332 text, with division notice p. [291] and epigraph p. [292]; p. [333] fly-title; p. [334] dedication; pp. 335–[426] text; pp. [427–8] blank.

Issued in purple cloth boards. Script blocked in gold foil across spine: Three | novels | by | Ronald | Firbank | Duckworth. Printed on white wove paper; white wove endpapers. All edges trimmed; top edge stained purple. Purple and white coated paper dust-jacket lettered in black and decorated in white, yellow, and black as designed by Keith Vaughan.

Published 30 November 1950 at 18*s*.; 6,000 copies were printed, of which 2,500 were bound and 3,500 exported in sheets for American issue. The British Library copy is dated 28 November 1961.

A second impression was released in November 1951 at 21*s*.; 2,000 copies were printed. This impression, uniform with that of 1950 except for appropriate revision of the publication notice p. [iv], was issued in yellow cloth boards with script blocked in gold foil on a purple background across the spine. Dust-jacket as described above.

e. Omnibus edition, American issue (1949–51):

The American issue of both volumes consisted of imported sheets uniform with collation and contents of the English issue except as noted below.

Volume I. *Five Novels:*

Demy 8°. $8\frac{1}{2}"\times 5\frac{1}{2}"$. xxxii, 480 pp.

All copies contain an altered title-leaf so that the recto (p. [iii]), the title-page, lacks publisher's device and the publisher's imprint reads, 'A New Directions Book'; on the verso (p. [iv]) are reservation of rights, note on the introduction, 'The Introduction by Osbert Sitwell is from | his forthcoming book, NOBLE ESSENCES, | to be published by the Atlantic Monthly Press', and combined publication and

A. BOOKS AND PAMPHLETS

imprint notice, 'New Directions Books are published by James Laughlin | Norfolk, Connecticut | Printed in Great Britain.' The last signature, S, is complete with pp. [473-80] blank.

Issued simultaneously so far as the publisher can ascertain in aqua cloth boards lettered in dark green across spine or in light aqua cloth boards lettered in gilt across spine: FIVE | [rule] | NOVELS | [rule] | BY | [rule] | RONALD | [rule] | FIRBANK | [rule] | NEW | [rule] | DIRECTIONS | [rule]. Cream white wove endpapers of stock heavier than text paper. All edges trimmed. Aqua and white dust-jacket lettered in black and decorated in white, grey, pink, and black.

Published November 1949 at $5. According to the publisher this impression consisted of 5,046 copies, although Duckworth states that sheets for only 5,000 copies were exported. New Directions names 21 November 1949 as date of release. If that is correct, then the American publication preceded the British. Noted by *The New York Times Book Review*, 20 November 1949; *Time*, 21 November 1949; *Publishers' Weekly*, 3 December 1949. The Library of Congress copy is dated 10 November 1949.

A subsequent impression was issued in August 1950, when 1,023 sheets were bound and the remaining 2,477 of 3,500 imported plus the 500 received from Duckworth's third impression were stocked for binding as needed. The imprint p. [iv] of the 1950 impression reads, 'Published by James Laughlin, Norfolk, Connecticut, | by arrangement with Coward, McCann, Inc. | Printed in Great Britain'; the imprint p. [472] of the same impression reads, '*Printed in Great Britain by* | *Phototype Limited, London*.' The 1951 impression lacks the second imprint p. [472]. Both lack pp. [473-80].

Volume II. *Three Novels:*

Demy 8°. 8½" × 5½". xx, 428 pp.

All copies contain an altered title-leaf so that the recto (p. [iii]), the title-page, lacks publisher's device, and the publisher's imprint reads, 'A New Directions Book'; on the verso (p. [iv]) is reservation of rights and combined publication and imprint notice, 'Published by James Laughlin, Norfolk, Connecticut, | by arrangement with Coward McCann, Inc. | Printed in Great Britain.'

Issued in aqua cloth boards. Lettered in gilt across spine: THREE | [rule] | NOVELS | [rule] | BY | [rule] | RONALD | [rule] | FIRBANK | [rule] | NEW | [rule] | DIRECTIONS | [rule]. Cream white wove endpapers of stock heavier than text paper. All edges trimmed. Cream white coated paper dust-jacket lettered in black and pink as designed by Andrew Warhol; the dust-jacket reads, '3 more novels of Ronald Firbank'.

Published March 1951 at $5; 3,500 copies were imported in sheets, of which 3,430 were bound and offered for sale. Noted by *Publishers'*

A. BOOKS AND PAMPHLETS

Weekly, 31 March 1951; *The New Yorker*, 14 April 1951; *The Nation*, 21 April 1951. The Library of Congress copy is dated 25 June 1951.

f. Second omnibus edition, American issue (1969):
Of the two volumes which make up the Omnibus edition, only *Five Novels* was issued.

Volume I. *Five Novels:*
Crown 8°. $7\frac{7}{8}'' \times 5\frac{1}{4}''$. xxxii, 342 pp. and 10 pp. unnumbered.

All copies contain an altered title leaf so that the recto (p. [iii]), the title-page, has swelled rules instead of swelled, beaded rules and the sequence of novels differs from that of the first editions; the verso (p. [iv]) lacks the note on the introduction and on its lower third are copyright notices, Library of Congress Catalogue Card Number 49-48966, reservation of rights, notice of the first edition and combined publication and imprint notice, 'New Directions books are published for James Laughlin | by New Directions Publishing Corporation | 333 Sixth Avenue, New York 10014'. The introduction by Osbert Sitwell is a reissue, uniform with the introduction to the English and American editions of 1949. Texts of the novels are those of the first editions (*Prancing Nigger*'s incorporates all corrections listed in the errata sheet of the second printing [A10a]). The sequence of the novels is: *The Flower Beneath the Foot*, pp. 1-94; *Prancing Nigger*, pp. 95-145 (p. [146] blank); *Valmouth*, pp. 149-239 (p. [240] blank); *The Artificial Princess*, pp. 241-87 (p. [288] blank); *Concerning the Eccentricities of Cardinal Pirelli*, pp. 289-342. Four of the five leaves on the rectos of which appear fly-titles for each novel with versos blank plus a final blank leaf are unnumbered and are not included in the pagination. Only the leaf containing the fly-title for *Valmouth*, p. 147 (p. [148] blank) is included in the page-count. Chapter divisions in the novels are in Roman italics between typographical ornaments, which differ for each novel.

Issued in fuchsia cloth boards; lettering in purple across the spine uniform with that of the first American edition. Printed on cream white wove paper; cream white wove endpapers. All edges trimmed. White and fuchsia coated paper dust-jacket lettered in fuchsia and purple with black and grey decorations reproduced in half-tone; lower dust-jacket lists 'New Directions' "Selected Writings" & "Readers" ', printed in black.

Published 25 April 1969 at $7.50; New Directions reports that 'something between one and two thousand copies were issued'. No Library of Congress deposit was made.

A. BOOKS AND PAMPHLETS

A13   THE ARTIFICIAL PRINCESS   1934

a. First ordinary edition:

THE | ARTIFICIAL PRINCESS | by | RONALD FIRBANK | With an Introduction by | SIR COLERIDGE KENNARD | DUCKWORTH | 3, Henrietta Street, London, W.C.2. | 1934

Demy 8°. $8\frac{1}{2}''$ × $5\frac{3}{8}''$. 84 pp. (x and 74 pp. paginated 11-84).

P. [i] half-title; p. [ii] list of 'BOOKS BY | RONALD FIRBANK' and below $\frac{1}{8}''$ rule, notice of 'Ronald Firbank. *A Memoir* by Ifan Kyrle Fletcher'; p. [iii] title; p. [iv] publication notice, reservation of rights, and imprint, 'Printed by The De La More Press, Ltd., | Shropshire House, 2-10 Pancras Street, | London, W. C. 1'; p. [v] Contents; p. [vi] blank; pp. vii-x Introduction signed 'COLERIDGE KENNARD' and dated *'Tangiers*, 1934'; pp. 11-84 text.

Issued in purple cloth boards. Lettered in gilt along top $3''$ of spine, upward: THE ARTIFICIAL PRINCESS. Printed on cream white laid paper; cream white wove endpapers. All edges trimmed. Bright green wove paper dust-jacket lettered and decorated with ornamental border in black.

Published May 1934 at 6s.; 2,000 copies were printed. Noted by *Times Literary Supplement*, 10 May 1934; *The Bookseller*, 16 May 1934. The British Library copy is dated 3 May 1934.

Apparently Firbank had definite plans for publishing *The Artificial Princess* before his death, for he wrote to Van Vechten from Arcachon on 11 September 1925: 'My books, The Cardinal & The Artificial Princess, (which I hope will amuse you) shall be sent as soon as published.'

The time in which Firbank composed the book is uncertain. Each of two drafts of his unpublished preface (Ts 1a) gives a different date. One says the novel was written 'while preparing for the Cambridge "Littlego": (A.D. 1906)'; the other names 1910 instead of 1906. In either case it remained unfinished until after 22 June 1925. On 22 June Firbank wrote to Van Vechten that when he sorted his mother's papers following her death in the spring he found a number of his early writings; among them he listed *The Artificial Princess*. 'I must tell you . . .', he said, 'how delighted I am with a short novel (unfinished), The Artificial Princess, & which I believe you will like better than any thing else of mine —.' Pp. 82-4, following the sentence 'A merciful end . . .', include the part written after 22 June 1925.

b. First limited edition (1934):

THE | ARTIFICIAL PRINCESS | by | RONALD FIRBANK | With an Introduction by | SIR COLERIDGE KENNARD

A. BOOKS AND PAMPHLETS

| ILLUSTRATIONS BY | HUGH EASTON | CENTAUR PRESS | LONDON | 1934

Demy 8°. 8¾" × 5 11/16". 84 pp. (x and 74 pp. paginated 11–84), frontispiece, and 2 illustrations.

This edition was printed from the same plates as the ordinary edition (A13a), with a re-set title-leaf. Its contents are uniform with the ordinary edition's except for the following insertions and changes: the altered title-page; limitation notice, '*Of this edition* 60 *copies only have | been printed of which* 50 | *are for sale | This is No.* [*number written in black ink*]' and imprint, 'Printed for The Centaur Press | by The De La More Press, Ltd., | Shropshire House, 2–10 Pancras | Street, London, W. C. 1', p. [iv]; frontispiece, black and white half-tone on white coated paper with legend 'THE PEARLS ABOUT HER THROAT BOUND HER CLOSER | TO THE CROSS', tipped in facing p. [iii]; 2 illustrations, the first produced uniformly with frontispiece and the second in black and white line, on white coated paper with legends 'THE BARONESS WITH GREAT SWEETNESS OF MANNER | RETIED HIS SASH' and 'HIS HANDS SEEMED FULL OF STARS' tipped in facing pp. 74 and 81.

Issued in yellow buckram boards. Lettered in gilt along spine, upward: THE ARTIFICIAL PRINCESS BY RONALD FIRBANK. Printed on white laid paper watermarked 'CORINTHIAN FINE TEXT —'; white laid endpapers watermarked uniformly. All edges trimmed; top edge stained green. Grey laid paper dust-jacket watermarked with a crown and 'Abbey Mills | Greenfield' and lettered in black.

Published May 1934 probably at 10*s.* 6*d.*; 60 copies were printed.

The British Library copy is dated 10 May 1934.

The agreement between Duckworth and the Centaur Press, completed 2 February 1934, empowered the Centaur Press to issue its edition subsequent to Duckworth's at not less than 10*s.* 6*d.* a copy. This volume, also by agreement, was designed as an addition to the five-volume *Works*, 1928 (A12a; cf. p. 41).

The records of the Centaur Press are not available. A letter from Hugh Easton dated 15 January 1961 states that, according to his recollection, Lady Kennard solicited his drawings and Louis Golding approved them. Easton did not see proofs before publication.

A14   A LETTER FROM ARTHUR RONALD   1934
        FIRBANK TO MADAME ALBANI

First edition:

A LETTER | From ARTHUR RONALD FIRBANK | To | MADAME ALBANI | Written about 1902–3. | And found

A. BOOKS AND PAMPHLETS

amongst her papers after | her death. | 50 *Facsimile Copies of this Letter have been printed by the Centaur Press, London, at five shillings net.*

Small Folio. 6¾" × 4½". [4] pp.

Pp. [1-3] text in facsimile with p. [1] plate marked at upper right: 'THE COOPERS, | CHISLEHURST.'; p. [4] blank.

Issued in envelope, 5" × 7", of grey laid paper watermarked with a crown and 'Abbey Mills | Greenfield' and lettered as above in black. On the envelope flap is hand-lettered in black ink: No. [*number added with rule approximately 1" drawn diagonally below*]. Printed on heavy white wove paper. Top and fore edge deckle; bottom edge trimmed. Publication date is unknown. It is designated as 1934, because every book recorded as issued by the Centaur Press appeared in 1934. The press may have operated, however, at least until 1936. (Cf. *The Manchester Public Libraries Reference Library Subject Catalogue Section 094 Private Press Books*, Part 1, edited by Sidney Horrocks, Manchester, 1959, pp. 13-14.) 50 copies were printed for sale at 5s. each.

A15　　　　　　　EXTRAVAGANZAS　　　　　　　1935

First edition:

EXTRAVAGANZAS | Containing | THE ARTIFICIAL PRINCESS | and | CONCERNING | THE ECCENTRICITIES OF | CARDINAL PIRELLI | By Ronald Firbank | NEW YORK | Coward-McCann | 1935

Crown 8°. 7⅜" × 5⅛". 208 pp.

P. [1] half-title; p. [2] blank; p. [3] title; p. [4] reservation of rights and imprint, 'PRINTED IN UNITED STATES OF AMERICA'; p. [5] Contents; p. [6] blank; pp. 7-11 Introduction, with 'INTRODUCTION' as a running head pp. 8-11, signed 'COLERIDGE KENNARD' and dated '*Tangiers*, 1934.'; p. [12] blank; p. [13] fly-title; p. [14] blank; pp. 14-101 text; p. [102] blank; p. [103] fly-title; p. [104] blank; pp. 105-204 text; pp. [205-8] blank.

Issued in black cloth boards. Lettered in gilt on upper cover: *Extravaganzas* [*decorative letters within double parentheses*, the *outer encasing the inner ones*] | RONALD FIRBANK; across spine at head: RONALD | FIRBANK and at foot: COWARD | McCANN; along centre of spine, downward: *Extravaganzas* [*decorative letters*]. Printed on cream white wove paper with cream white wove endpapers of lighter stock. Top edge trimmed; other edges rough trimmed. Beige wove paper dust-jacket lettered and decorated in purple. The dust-jacket lists *The Artificial Princess* as 'The Enchanted Princess'.

A. BOOKS AND PAMPHLETS

Published November 1935 at $2; 1,200 copies were printed of which 230 were sold. Noted by *Publishers' Weekly*, 9 November 1935; *The New York Times*, 17 November 1935, *Boston Evening Transcript*, 23 November 1935. The Library of Congress copy is dated 28 March 1936.

The introduction is a reprint of the introduction to *The Artificial Princess* (A13a). Texts are those of the first editions (A13a and A11).

A16   LA PRINCESSE ARTIFICIELLE   1938
SUIVI DE MON PIAFFEUR NOIR

First edition:

RONALD FIRBANK | LA PRINCESSE | ARTIFICIELLE | *Traduit de l'anglais par Maurice Sachs* | SUIVI DE | MON PIAFFEUR NOIR | *traduit par E. Roditi* | [*monogram of La Nouvelle Revue Française*] | Gallimard | Paris-43, rue de Beaune | S.P.

Crown 8°. $7\frac{3}{8}'' \times 4\frac{5}{8}''$. 224 pp.

Pp. [1-2] blank; p. [3] half-title; p. [4] blank; p. [5] title; p. [6] blank; p. [7] fly-title and dedication, '*Cette traduction est respectueusement | et amicalement dédiée* | à MADAME YVONNE PRINTEMPS | M. S., 1937.'; p. [8] blank; pp. [9]-108 text; p. [109] fly-title; p. [110] blank; pp. [111]-219 text; p. [220] blank; p. [221] Contents; p. [222] blank; p. [223] imprint, '[*rule*] | PARIS – SOCIÉTÉ GÉNÉRALE | D'IMPRIMERIE ET D'ÉDITION, | 71, RUE DE RENNES. – 1938 | [*rule*]'; p. [224] blank.

Issued in cream paper covers. Single-rule black frame enclosing double-rule red frame and lettered in black and red (titles of the novels) on upper cover: RONALD FIRBANK | LA PRINCESSE | ARTIFICIELLE | *Traduit de l'anglais par Maurice Sachs* | SUIVI DE | MON PIAFFEUR NOIR | *traduit par E. Roditi* | [*monogram of La Nouvelle Revue Française*] | GALLIMARD | S. P. [*outside both frames*]; across spine: RONALD | FIRBANK | LA | PRINCESSE | ARTIFICIELLE | [*monogram of La Nouvelle Revue Française*] | GALLIMARD with black single-rule and red double-rule at head and tail. On the lower cover is a list of 'EDITIONS DE LA | NOUVELLE REVUE FRANÇAISE' dated 1937. Printed on cream wove paper. All edges rough trimmed. Transparent paper dust-jacket.

Published July or August 1938 at 18 Fr.; 3,300 copies were printed. Gallimard can provide no information as to exact date of publication, because such records disappeared during the German Occupation. Announced in Gallimard's monthly catalogue in *La Nouvelle Revue Française*, 1 August 1938, as 'Vient de Paraître'.

A. BOOKS AND PAMPHLETS

No other translation of Firbank's novels was published until 1962, although from time to time several were under consideration. On 30 October 1924 Montgomery Evans, a young American travelling in Europe (he had met Firbank in Paris), wrote from Prague saying that Emerick Reeck of Frankfurt wanted to put *Prancing Nigger* (A10a) into German. (Unpublished letter, Firbank family papers.) Reeck, who sometimes published under the pseudonym Hyazinth Lehmann, had already made successful translations from English. Firbank promptly completed the necessary arrangements with him. And on 16 December 1924 Firbank told Stuart Rose that the translation of *Prancing Nigger* was under way with 'Valmouth (A6a) to follow'. No record of publication can be found. In late 1929, probably in November, William A. Bradley, then living in Paris, opened negotiations for an unnamed person in an attempt to arrange for a translation of *Prancing Nigger* into French. Correspondence with Brentano's produced no agreement. Bompiani S. A. – Editrice, Rome, investigated the possibility of publishing an Italian translation of *Prancing Nigger* and *The Artificial Princess* (A13a). That was in April 1946. Again no agreement was concluded.

A17   THE COMPLETE RONALD FIRBANK   1961

a. First edition, English issue:

The Complete | RONALD FIRBANK | With a preface by | ANTHONY POWELL | [*publisher's device*] | GERALD DUCKWORTH & CO. LTD. | 3 Henrietta Street, London, W. C. 2 [*within a triple-rule and floral frame*]

Crown 8°. $7\frac{3}{4}'' \times 5\frac{1}{16}''$. ii, 768 pp.

P. [i] half-title on recto of white coated paper leaf, tipped in, and photograph of Firbank with autograph signature and date 1917 reproduced in black and white half-tone with legend 'RONALD FIRBANK' on verso p. [ii]; p. [1] title; p. [2] publication and copyright notices and imprint, 'MADE AND PRINTED IN GREAT BRITAIN BY | THE GARDEN CITY PRESS LIMITED | LETCHWORTH, HERTFORDSHIRE'; p. [3] Contents; p. [4] blank; pp. 5-[16] Preface signed 'ANTHONY POWELL'; pp. 17-765 text with pp. 26, 74, 318, 478, and 644 blank; p. 766 dedications as in first editions of *Odette* (A4), *Caprice* (A5), and *The Flower Beneath the Foot* (A9a); pp. [767-8] blank.

Issued in black cloth boards. On upper cover in gilt, facsimile of Firbank's early signature: A. A. R. Firbank; lettered in gilt across spine: THE COMPLETE | RONALD FIRBANK [*within triple-rule boxed gilt frame*] | DUCKWORTH. Printed on white wove paper with light blue wove endpapers of heavier stock. All edges trimmed;

A. BOOKS AND PAMPHLETS

top edge stained blue. Cream paper dust-jacket lettered in blue and black and decorated with black and white half-tone reproduction of portrait by Augustus John.

Published 27 April 1961 at 42s.; the publisher estimates that 5,100 copies were printed.

The texts of *Santal* and *The Artificial Princess* are those of the first editions (A8a and A13a); the texts of all other titles are those of *The Works* (A12a) with minor corrections.

b. First edition, American issue (1961):

On 25 October 1961 New Directions offered 350 imported copies of the first edition for sale in America at $7.75 the copy. New Directions stamped its imprint below Duckworth's on the title page. The shilling price was clipped from the inside flap of the upper dust-jacket, and the dollar price and 'Distributed by New Directions' stamped in. All this was done by hand.

On 17 December 1962 or shortly thereafter New Directions offered another 1,000 imported copies for sale at $8.25 the copy. These represented a second impression. The second is uniform with the first except that on the title-page, p. [1], 'A NEW DIRECTIONS BOOK' replaces Duckworth's name and device and to p. [2] is added, after the publication notice, 'Second Impression 1962' and, after the copyright notice, 'New Directions Books are published at | Norfolk, Connecticut, by James Laughlin. | New York Office: 333 Sixth Avenue (14)'. On the spine 'DUCKWORTH' is replaced by 'NEW | DIRECTIONS'. New Direction's name also appears on the dust-jacket; advertising matter differs, and the dollar price is printed on the inside flap of the upper dust-jacket.

A18   PENGUIN MODERN CLASSICS EDITION   1961

RONALD FIRBANK | [*swelled rule*] | *Valmouth* | *Prancing Nigger* | *Concerning the Eccentricities* | *of Cardinal Pirelli* | Penguin Books

Foolscap 8°. $7\frac{1}{8}''$ × $4\frac{5}{16}''$. 256 pp.

P. [1] half-title, publisher's device, a 25-line bio-bibliographical note on Firbank, and note on portrait reproduced on upper cover; p. [2] blank; p. [3] title; p. [4] publisher's imprint, publication notes on each title and on the volume, copyright notice, note on *The Complete Ronald Firbank* (A17), and imprint, 'Made and printed in Great Britain | by Cox & Wyman Ltd, | London, Reading, and Fakenham'; p. [5] Contents; p. [6] blank; p. [7] fly-title; p. [8] blank; pp. 9–[116] text; p. [117] fly-title; p. [118] blank; pp. 119–[83] text;

A. BOOKS AND PAMPHLETS

p. [184] blank; p. [185] fly-title; p. [186] blank; pp. 187-[251] text; p. [252] blank; pp. [253-6] integral publisher's catalogue.

Issued in grey glazed stiff paper wrappers lettered and decorated in black, a portrait by Augustus John produced in half-tone, and black bands lettered in white, with a black and white publisher's device against an orange background on both wrappers.

Published simultaneously with *The Complete Ronald Firbank* (A17) 27 April 1961 as Penguin Book No. 1570 at 3s. 6d.; the publisher is unwilling to disclose the number of copies printed.

A19   THE NEW RYTHUM AND OTHER PIECES   1962

a. First edition:

THE NEW RYTHUM | AND OTHER PIECES | by | RONALD FIRBANK | [*publisher's device*] | GERALD DUCKWORTH & CO. LTD. | 3 Henrietta Street, London, W.C.2

Demy 8°. $8\frac{1}{2}'' \times 5\frac{1}{2}''$. 136 pp., frontispiece, and 14 illustrations.

P. [1] half-title; p. [2] blank; frontispiece, portrait photograph reproduced in black and white half-tone with legend 'RONALD FIRBANK | *photographed by Elliott and Fry in* 1917' on text paper sewed, facing p. [3]; p. [3] title; p. [4] publication notice, copyright notices, and imprint, 'PRINTED IN GREAT BRITAIN | BY EBENEZER BAYLIS AND SON, LTD. | THE TRINITY PRESS, WORCESTER, AND LONDON'; p. [5] Contents; p. [6] blank; pp. [7-8] List of Illustrations; pp. 9-17 Introduction signed 'ALAN HARRIS'; p. [18] blank; p. [19] fly-title, '*A Study in Temperament* | ARTHUR ANNESLEY RONALD FIRBANK'; p. [20] blank; pp. 21-9 text; p. [30] blank; p. [31] fly-title, '*Lady Appledore's Mésalliance* | AN ARTIFICIAL PASTORAL | by | A. A. R. FIRBANK'; p. [32] blank; pp. 33-67 text; p. [68] blank; p. [69] fly-title, '*The New Rythum* | by | RONALD FIRBANK'; p. [70] blank; pp. 71-112 text including, pp. 108-112, '*Extracts from the Notebooks*'; p. [113] fly-title, '*A Miscellany*'; p. [114] blank; pp. 115-[26] text of 'A MISCELLANY OF SHORT PASSAGES | FROM UNPUBLISHED WRITING'; pp. 127-[35] Appendix; p. [136] advertisement within single-rule black frame. Fourteen illustrations produced uniformly with the frontispiece are printed on text paper with legends: 'HEATHER AND RONALD FIRBANK | *a nursery photograph, date unknown*' and 'RONALD FIRBANK | *photo by Lavender of Bromley, no date*' between pp. 14 and 15; '*Signed* ARTHUR FIRBANK, 1905', 'RONALD FIRBANK | *photographed by Kaulak, Madrid*, 1905' (the legend for two consecutive illustrations), and '*A page from* IDEAS & FANCIES, 1904' between pp. 56 and 57; '*Page 8 from the* Daily Mirror *of February 5th*, 1908. The

A. BOOKS AND PAMPHLETS

fourth starter | *from the left in the top picture is Ronald Firbank*', '*A view of Firbank's room at Trinity Hall, Cambridge,* 1907', '*Another view of the same*', and 'RONALD | FIRBANK | *on a Nile* | *house-boat,* | *no date*' between pp. 88 and 89; 'LADY FIRBANK | *Ronald's mother, no date*', '*Facsimile double-page spread from the notebooks of* THE NEW RYTHUM', and 'RONALD FIRBANK | *photographed by Bertram Park,* 1917' between pp. 104 and 105. Each group of illustrations is on conjugate leaves except those on the one leaf between pp. 14 and 15; that leaf is conjugate with the frontispiece leaf. All are sewed.

Issued in red quarter cloth and beige paper boards decorated with a facsimile reproduction of pages from the notebooks for 'The New Rythum'; lettered in gilt across spine: RONALD | FIRBANK | [*asterisk*] | THE | NEW | RYTHUM | and | other | pieces | DUCKWORTH. Printed on white wove paper; pink laid endpapers with indecipherable watermark. All edges trimmed; top edge stained red. Beige and red paper dust-jacket lettered in red on beige and beige on red and decorated with reproduction of facsimile on covers.

Published 26 July 1962 at 21*s.*; 5,000 copies were printed. The British Library copy is dated 19 July 1962.

The text of 'A Study in Temperament' (pp. [19]-29) is that of the first edition (A1a). The text of 'Lady Appledore's Mésalliance' (pp. [31]-67) is that of Ts 6. (Cf. C9.) The text of 'Impression d'Automne' (p. 116) is an excerpt from the 'prose poem' printed as 'Souvenir d'Automne' (C3).

No other work included in this volume has hitherto been published. Nor did Firbank intend that any should be except 'The New Rythum' (pp. [69]-107). The others he dismissed as juvenilia when he found them among his mother's papers after her death in the spring of 1925. As he told Van Vechten at that time, he was 'glad' to have had 'the tact as a child not to rush headlong into print'.

'The New Rythum' is another matter. Though incomplete, it belongs to the sequence of novels which Firbank turned out, one after the other, in the twenties. As might be expected, he had a plan for it even before he started to write its predecessor *Cardinal Pirelli* (A11). In early September 1923 he first mentioned it and said that he 'pined' to begin the 'American novel'. But he did not actually do so until more than two years had passed. According to a letter which he sent Grant Richards from Shepheard's Hotel, Cairo, Firbank began 'The New Rythum' on the morning of 1 November 1925. Six weeks later he told Van Vechten about this book with his private vision of New York and Palm Beach 'for setting'. After describing how he set up a parasol and a 'little French writing table' in the desert every morning, Firbank said that he sat and pictured the American scene in the mirage. 'So beautiful & poetic it seems some times,' he wrote, 'I begin to love it — especially Harlem. I am evolving a divine negress Aunt Andromeda & her friend — Mrs. Storykoff, married to a Pole who runs a dope-den off Grammercy Park.' These characters were

A. BOOKS AND PAMPHLETS

apparently a part of the mirage and did not materialize, but Firbank continued to work at others in 'The New Rythum' after he went to Rome in the spring. When he died in May, he had written six chapters and part of a seventh.

The text of the appendix (pp. 127-[35]) is an abbreviated version of Sotheby & Co.'s catalogue (pp. [3]-27, B4) of the Firbank papers which were offered for sale on 12 December 1961.

b. First edition, American issue (1963):

On 30 April 1963, New Directions offered for sale in America 1,000 imported copies of the first edition at $5.25 the copy. The American issue is uniform with the English issue with the following exceptions. 'A NEW DIRECTIONS BOOK' replaces the publisher's device and Duckworth's name and address on the title (p.3). To p. [4] is added 'Library of Congress Catalogue No. 63-8814' and 'New Directions Books are published by | James Laughlin at Norfolk, Connecticut | New York office – 333 Sixth Avenue (14)'. On both spine and dust-jacket, 'New Directions' appears instead of 'Duckworth'. On the inside flap of the upper dust-jacket is added advertising matter and 'A NEW DIRECTIONS BOOK'; the shilling price is replaced with $5.25. The advertising matter on the inside flap of the lower dust-jacket of the American issue also differs from that of the English issue, and the name and address of New Directions is added.

A.19.1 VANAGLORIA 1962

First edition:

Ronald Firbank | Vanagloria [*large brown decorative letters*] | Rizzoli

Crown 8°. $8\frac{9}{16}'' \times 5\frac{1}{2}''$. 268 pp.

P. [1] series title and at lower left corner '1. Vanagloria'; p. [2] blank; p. [3] title; p. [4] reservation of rights, notice of original title and of the translator; pp. 5-[13] Introduction signed 'Laura Lovisetti Fuà'; p. [14] identification of characters and place names in English and Italian; pp. 15-[264] text; pp. [265-6] Contents; p. [267] publication notice: '*Finito di stampare il 12-9-1962 | nello stabilimento di Rizzoli Editore in Milano*' and imprint, 'Printed in Italy'; p. [268] blank.

Issued in white cloth boards with multicoloured peacock-tail design on top two-thirds of upper cover and spine and entire lower cover. Lettered in black on white third of upper cover: '*romanzo di* | RONALD FIRBANK | RIZZOLI | VANAGLORIA' [letters $\frac{9}{16}''$ in height]. Printed on white wove paper; white wove endpapers. All

A. BOOKS AND PAMPHLETS

edges trimmed. With cream white and dark blue wrap-around band, $\frac{7}{16}''$ in width, lettered in white on blue 'Perché signora Shamefoot vuol essere vetrificata?' and in blue on white in small letters 'Vanagloria'. Transparent plastic dust-jacket.

Published 12 September 1962 at L.2000. The number of copies issued is not available.

A20   NEW DIRECTIONS PAPERBOOK EDITION   1962

RONALD FIRBANK | Two Novels | The Flower | Beneath The Foot | Prancing Nigger | With A Chronology | *by Miriam K. Benkovitz* | A NEW DIRECTIONS PAPERBOOK

Crown 8°. $7\frac{1}{16}'' \times 4\frac{1}{4}''$. [iv], 348 pp. (paginated 9–356).

P. [i] title; p. [ii] Contents, copyright notice, reservation of rights, Library of Congress catalogue card number, publication notices, and imprint, 'Manufactured in the United States of America | Printed by The Murray Printing Company | New Directions Books are published by James Laughlin at | Norfolk, Connecticut. New York Office: 333 Sixth Avenue (14).'; p. [iii] fly-title, 'The Flower | Beneath the Foot | *Being a Record of the Early Life of* | *St. Laura de Nazianzi and the* | *Times in Which She Lived*'; p. [iv] epigraphs; pp. 9–224 text; p. [225] fly-title, 'Prancing Nigger'; p. [226] blank; pp. 227–350 text with p. [230] blank; pp. 351-6 '*A Chronology of Ronald Firbank*' signed 'Miriam J. Benkovitz'.

Issued in white glazed stiff paper wrappers lettered in black and grey on white and white on black of decorative photograph produced in black and white half-tone on upper wrapper. Advertisement on lower wrapper and list of New Directions Paperbooks inside both wrappers. Printed on white wove paper. All edges trimmed.

Published 31 October 1962 as New Directions Paperbook 128 at $1.90; 10,000 copies were printed.

The texts of both novels are re-impressions by photolithography of those of the first editions (A9a and A10a).

A21   "THE WIND & THE ROSES"   [1966]

First edition:

"THE WIND | & THE ROSES" | RONALD | FIRBANK | With an Introduction by | Miriam J. Benkovitz | privately | printed | for Alan Clodd | 1965

A. BOOKS AND PAMPHLETS

Royal 8°. $9\frac{7}{16}''\times 6''$. [12] pp.

P. [1] title; p. [2] reservation of rights; pp. [3-5] introduction; p. [6] blank; p. [7] fly-title; p. [8] blank; pp. 9-[10] text; p. [11] limitation notice, '*50 copies of this edition | have been printed | of which this is number . . . [number written in blue ink]*' and imprint, '*John Roberts Press Limited | London*'; p. [12] blank.

Issued in lavender laid paper wrappers, $10''\times 6\frac{1}{2}''$, with folding flaps pasted to white stiff glazed paper wrappers sewn with the single gathering. Lettered in purple on upper wrapper: RONALD FIRBANK | A | POEM | "THE | WIND & THE | ROSES" [*in decorative letters*]; drawing by Aubrey Beardsley (first published in *The Pierrot of the Minute* by Ernest Dowson, 1897) reproduced in line on upper wrapper. Printed on cream Basingwerk Parchment. All edges trimmed.

Issued 15 January 1966; none was for sale although a few were offered at £2.5s. Seventy copies were printed of which fifty were numbered 1 to 50 and the remainder i to xx, *hors commerce*. The British Library copy is dated 30 April 1966.

The text is that of Firbank's holograph, Ms 13.

A22   FAR AWAY   1966

First edition:

RONALD FIRBANK | FAR AWAY [*in large purple decorative letters*] | NOW FIRST PRINTED WITH A | BIOBIBLIOGRAPHICAL NOTE | BY MIRIAM J. BENKOVITZ | Typographic Laboratory | University of Iowa

4°. $9\frac{15}{16}''\times 4\frac{1}{2}''$. [12] pp.

P. [1] title; p. [2] reservation of rights and limitation notice, 'One hundred copies printed from | Van Dijck type on Carousel paper'; p. [3] note on the text and acknowledgement signed 'M. J. B.'; p. [4] blank; pp. [5-7] text; p. [8] blank; pp. [9-12] note signed 'Miriam J. Benkovitz'.

Issued in yellow laid paper wrappers. Lettered in purple on upper wrapper: Far Away | [*typographical ornament*]. The two initial leaves and the two final leaves, conjugate, printed on pale blue laid paper and the two centre leaves, conjugate, printed on yellow laid paper, all watermarked: HAMILTON CAROUSEL. The entire booklet, including wrappers, is sewn with purple thread. Upper wrapper and some final leaves, deckle; other edges trimmed.

Issued 13 April 1966. None was for sale. According to Harry Duncan, who oversaw production of the booklet, 20 copies were spoiled in production so that only 80 were issued. No Library of Congress deposit was made.

A. BOOKS AND PAMPHLETS

The text is that of "Far Away" (Ms 1) with capitalization and the use of dashes regularized.

A23　　　　　　　INCLINAZIONI　　　　　　　1966

First edition:

Ronald Firbank [*in large purple letters*] | Inclinazioni | *Vallecchi Editore*

Demy 8°. 8½" × 5⅜". 172 pp.

Pp. [1-2] blank; p. [3] series title and number: '*Narratori Vallechi* 24'; p. [4] blank; p. [5] half-title; p. [6] Notice of translation: 'Traduzione italiana | di Laura Lovisetti Fuà | Titolo originale: "Inclinations" ', and copyright notice; p. [7] title; p. [8] blank; p. [9] fly-title with division notice and epigraph; p. [10] blank; pp. 11-110 text; p. [111] fly-title with division notice and epigraph; p. [112] blank; pp. 113-50 text; p. [151] fly-title, '*APPENDICE*'; p. [152] note on appendix, 'Diamo qui, in appendice, la seconda versione (datata: Roma, | aprile 1925) del capitola IV, parte seconda.'; pp. [153-63] text; p. [164] blank; p. [165] fly-title, 'INDICE'; p. [166] blank; pp. [167-8] table of contents; p. [169] imprint and publication notice, 'Finito di stampare | presso le Officine Grafiche | Vallecchi Editore di Firenze | nel maggio 1966'; p. [170] blank; p. [171] list of twenty-four 'Narratori Vallecchi'; p. [172] blank.

Issued in white stiff paper wrappers. Lettered in black on upper wrapper: Ronald Firbank | Inclinazioni | VALLECCHI EDITORE FIRENZE; on upper half of spine, upward: Ronald Firbank Inclinazioni. Tipped in inside lower cover is a 3¾" square white label lettered in black with author, title, publisher, price and typographical ornament. Printed on white wove paper. All edges trimmed. White coated paper dust-jacket lettered in black and purple and decorated with reproduction in black and white of Henry Matisse's *Nude in Armchair*; purple spine lettered in black and white. Inside flaps of the dust-jacket contain a critical statement about *Inclinations* and Firbank's other works and a short biography. The upper flap also identifies Matisse's *Nude* and the designer of the dust-jacket and typography, Bob Noorda.

Published 24 May 1966 as Vallecchi novel 24 at L. 1500; the number of copies issued is not available.

The appendix is a translation of the revised dinner party chapter first printed in *The Works of Ronald Firbank*, Vol. II, pp. 133-41 (A12a).

A. BOOKS AND PAMPHLETS

A24   AN EARLY FLEMISH PAINTER   1969

First edition:

AN EARLY | FLEMISH | PAINTER | RONALD FIRBANK [*within black decorative frame*]
Crown 8°. 7⅜" × 4 13/16". [8] pp.
P. [1] title; p. [2] reservation of rights, acknowledgement, and production notice: 'Printed and made in Great Britain'; p. [3] Introductory note signed 'Miriam J. Benkovitz'; p. [4] frontispiece, portrait of Emperor Charles V attributed to Jan Gossaert, reproduced in black and white half-tone, within single-rule grey frame on coated paper, tipped in; pp. [5-7] text; p. [8] publication notice: 'Issued at Christmas 1969 as a greeting for the friends of the | Enitharmon Press and Miriam J. Benkovitz'; and imprint: 'Printed by Daedalus Press, Stoke Ferry, Norfolk for the | Enitharmon Press, 22 Huntingdon Road, East Finchley, | London N. 2'.

Issued in purple stiff paper wrappers sewn with the single gathering. Lettered in black within black decorative frame on upper wrapper: SEASON'S | GREETINGS | *The* Enitharmon Press [or] Miriam J. Benkovitz. Printed on white laid paper. All edges trimmed.

Issued 22 November 1969; 300 copies were printed of which 185 had the name Enitharmon Press and 115, Miriam J. Benkovitz. None was for sale. The British Library copy is dated 23 February 1970.

The text is identical with that published in *The Academy* on 28 December 1907 (C5.1).

A25   DIE EXZENTRIZITÄTEN DES KARDINALS   1970
PIRELLI BETREFFEND

First edition:

Ronald Firbank | Die Exzentrizitäten | des Kardinals Pirelli | betreffend | Roman | Mit | einem Nachwort | von Arthur Waley | Carl Hanser | Verlag

Only one copy of this translation is known, and it was not available for examination. That copy is the property of Otto Oppertshäuser, who transcribed the title page.

A26   TWO EARLY STORIES   1971

First edition:

TWO EARLY | STORIES | by | Ronald Firbank | *foreword by Miriam J. Benkovitz* | *Illustrations by Edward Gorey* |

A. BOOKS AND PAMPHLETS

ALBONDOCANI PRESS : NEW YORK : 1971 [*within black decorative frame*]

Crown 8°. $7\frac{7}{16}'' \times 5\frac{1}{2}''$. 56 pp.

P. [1] title; p. [2] reservation of rights; p. [3] Contents; p. [4] blank; pp. [5]-7 Foreword signed 'Miriam J. Benkovitz'; p. [8] blank; p. [9] half-title; p. [10] blank; p. [11] fly-title, black and green line cut with 'THE WAVERING DISCIPLE' in the plate, on text paper; p. [12] blank; pp. [13]-27 text with tail-pieces, black and green line cuts on pp. 16 and 19, marking the ends of chapters 1 and 2; p. [28] blank; p. [29] fly-title, black and green line cut with 'A STUDY IN OPAL' in the plate, on text paper; p. [30] blank; pp. [31]-54 text with tail-piece, black and green line cut on p. 54; p. [55] colophon and limitation notice: '*This first edition of | TWO EARLY STORIES | published in May 1971 | is limited to | two hundred and twenty-six copies. | The type is Goudy, | the paper is Fabriano Text, | and the wrappers are | French marble paper. | Two hundred copies | numbered 1-200 are for sale. | Twenty-six copies | lettered A-Z for the use | of the publisher | are not for sale. | This is number [number written in black ink]*'; p. [56] imprint, 'Printed by William Ferguson | Cambridge, Massachusetts | Albondocani Press Publication No. 11'.

Issued in brown, grey and gold marbled paper wrappers, $7\frac{13}{16}'' \times 5\frac{3}{4}''$, with folding flaps over stiff paper wrappers with white verso and grey recto; pasted on the upper wrapper is a white label, $1\frac{3}{4}'' \times 2\frac{1}{2}''$, lettered in black: TWO EARLY STORIES | [*rule*] | RONALD FIR-BANK [*within black decorative frame*]. Printed on olive green laid paper watermarked 'Fabriano (Italy)'; olive green laid free end-papers, watermarked uniformly, integral with the text. Fore-edge deckle; other edges trimmed.

Published 15 June 1971 at $20; 235 copies were printed. No Library of Congress deposit was made.

Except for minor variations in the use of capital letters, the texts are identical with the texts which appeared in *The Granta*, 1906 and 1907 (C4-6).

A27   LA PRINCESSE AUX SOLEILS &   1974
              HARMONIE

First edition:

La Princesse aux Soliels | & | Harmonie | by | Ronald Firbank | with English versions by | EDGELL RICKWORD | and an Introductory Note by | MIRIAM J. BENKOVITZ | Illustrated by Philippe Jullian | London . ENITHARMON PRESS . 1974

61

A. BOOKS AND PAMPHLETS

4°. $9\frac{5}{8}'' \times 6\frac{1}{8}''$. xviii, 14 pp.

Pp. [i–ii] blank; p. [iii] half-title; p. [iv] blank; p. [v] title; p. [vi] publication notice, reservation of rights, SBN 901111 43 0, and production notice, 'Printed and made in Great Britain'; pp. [vii–viii] blank; p. [ix] illustration, black and white line cut on text paper; p. [x] blank; pp. [xi–xiii] Introduction; p. [xiv] blank; p. [xv] fly-title; pp. [xvi–xviii] blank; pp. 1-2 French text; pp. 3-4 English text; p. [5] fly-title; pp. [6-8] blank; p. 9 French text; p. [10] blank; p. 11 English text; p. [12] blank; p. [13] limitation notice and colophon, '200 copies of LA PRINCESSE AUX SOLEILS and | HARMONIE have been printed by Daedalus Press | for the Enitharmon Press on Glastonbury Antique Laid paper | This is number | . . .' [number written in black ink], tail-piece, black and white line cut; p. [14] blank. Page numbers are printed within square brackets. Illustrations, black and white half-tones on the rectos of white coated conjugate leaves (versos blank), are inserted between pp. [xiv] and [xv] and between pp. [6] and [7].

Issued in black quarter cloth and purple boards; lettered in gilt along spine, downward: RONALD FIRBANK LA PRINCESSE AUX SOLEILS ENITHARMON. Printed on cream laid paper; pale yellow wove endpapers. All edges trimmed. Glassine dust-jacket.

Published 28 June 1974 at £5.25; 215 copies were printed of which 200 were meant for sale, but 30 copies were found to lack the terminal E in the word PRINCESSE on the spine and were withdrawn from sale. The British Library copy is dated 5 July 1974.

The French texts are identical with those which appeared in "*Les Essais*", 1904 and 1905 (C1-2).

A28   HET GRILLIGE LEVEN VAN KARDINAAL   1975 PIRELLI GEVOLGD DOOR VALMOUTH

First edition:

Ronald Firbank | Het grillige levan van | kardinaal Pirelli | *gevolgd door* | Valmouth | Vertaling en nawoord van Gerrit Komrij | Meulenhoff Amsterdam

Crown 8°. $7\frac{7}{8}'' \times 4\frac{7}{8}''$. 176 pp.

P. [1] half-title; p. [2] publisher's name: 'Meulenhoff Editie'; p. [3] title; p. [4] Note on English titles, copyright notices, notes on design for upper cover and graphic designer, imprint, 'Druk: Van Boekhoven-Bosch bv, Utrecht', and ISBN 90 290 0179 8; p. [5] Contents; p. [6] blank; p. [7] fly-title; pp. 8-70 text; p. [71] fly-title; pp. 72-170 text; pp. 171-5 Afterword signed 'Gerrit Komrij'; p. 176 Bibliography.

A. BOOKS AND PAMPHLETS

Issued in white glazed stiff paper wrappers lettered in purple on upper wrapper: Het grillige | leven van | kardinaal Pirelli; and in green: Door | Ronald | Firbank | Vertaling en nawoord van | Gerrit Konrij. Mustard yellow spine lettered in black across head: M; across tail: E364; centre of spine downward: Ronald Firbank . Het grillige levan van Kardinaal Pirelli. Detail of a design for wallpaper by Walter Crane, 'This is the house that Jack Built', reproduced in half-tone in mustard yellow, orange, green, and blue on upper wrapper. Photograph of Firbank, half-tone; a critical comment on his work with quotations from Evelyn Waugh, Jocelyn Brooke, Edmund Wilson, and Cyril Connolly; publisher's logogram and name and ISB number on lower wrapper.

Published 27 June 1975 at Dfl. 18.50; 3,000 copies were printed.

A29   WHEN WIDOWS LOVE & A TRAGEDY   1980
IN GREEN TWO STORIES

First edition:

RONALD FIRBANK | [*rule broken at centre by three beaded diamonds*] | WHEN WIDOWS LOVE | & | A TRAGEDY IN GREEN [*in decorative letters*] | [*rule broken at centre by three beaded diamonds*] | TWO STORIES | *Edited and Introduced by* | Edward Martin Potoker | The Bernard M. Baruch College | of the City University of New York | LONDON | THE ENITHARMON PRESS | 1980

Royal 8°. $9\frac{7}{8}'' \times 6\frac{7}{8}''$. 44 pp.

P. [1] half-title; p. [2] blank; p. [3] title; p. [4] publication notice, ISBN 0 905289 06 4, limitation notice, copyright notices, publisher's acknowledgements, and imprint '*Printed and Made in Great Britain by* | *Skelton's Press Wellingborough Northants*'; p. [5] 'NOTE AND ACKNOWLEDGMENTS' signed 'E. M. P.'; p. [6] blank; p. [7] Contents; p. [8] dedication, '*To My Parents* | *Bessie and Benjamin Potoker*'; pp. 4-14 Introduction signed 'EDWARD MARTIN POTOKER' and dated '*New York, N.Y.* | *July 18, 1978*'; p. [15] fly-title; p. [16] blank; pp. 17-24 text; p. [25] fly-title; p. [26] dedication, 'TO | THE INSPIRER OF THE TRAGEDY | SIR COLERIDGE KENNARD' and introductory exchange between Pierrot and Pierette; p. 27-[36] text; p. [37] fly-title, 'APPENDIX | *A letter from Ronald Firbank to* | *Carl Van Vechten 22 June 1925*'; p. [38] blank; pp. [39-41] facsimile of letter; pp. [42-4] blank.

Issued in maroon, coarse-spun linen boards lettered in gilt on spine downward: Ronald Firbank TWO STORIES Enitharmon. Printed

A. BOOKS AND PAMPHLETS

on white wove paper; sea-green wove endpapers of heavier stock watermarked: 'John Bullen' with occasional flowers of five petals. All edges trimmed. Pale yellow laid paper dust-jacket watermarked with a crown and 'Abbey Mills | Greenfield'. Upper jacket lettered in black script incorporated in a line drawing by Frances Richards reproduced in black; black script on the spine; lower cover and inner flap of upper cover lettered in black.

Published 28 May 1980 at £8.50; 300 copies were printed.

The texts are those of the typescripts (Ts 13 and Ts 11) with spelling regularized.

Twenty copies contain a cancel title-leaf (pp. [3-4]). The cancel was necessitated by the fact that, after the sheets had been delivered for binding, twenty copies were found to lack a copyright page. For these twenty copies, a new title-leaf with copyright and other information on its verso (p. [4]) was then prepared and inserted on a stub with its conjugate leaf (pp. 13-14).

This book had gone to press when, in the spring of 1981, the second omnibus edition, American issue, of *Five Novels* (A12f) was reissued as a New Directions Paperbook 518. It is uniform with the issue of 1969 with these exceptions: the half-title (p. [1]) lacks the author's name; on the verso of the title leaf (p. [iv]) are copyright notices, reservation of rights, notes on manufacture and publication, and imprint showing the publisher's change of address to '80 Eighth Avenue, New York 10011. Issued in stiff white coated paper covers; on upper cover is a photograph of 'Countess Castiolione' reproduced in black and white and, across the bottom inch of the cover between double rules, 'FIVE NOVELS · RONALD FIRBANK'; along spine downward, 'RONALD FIRBANK FIVE NOVELS NDP 518'. On lower cover are ISB number, title and author, a discussion of Firbank's work, acknowledgment for the photograph on upper cover, publisher's name, paperbook number, and price, $7.95. Printed on white wove paper of lighter stock than the issue of 1969. Number of copies issued is unknown.

B.
CONTRIBUTIONS TO BOOKS AND PAMPHLETS

B1 PILLORIED! 1928

First edition:

PILLORIED! [*in large decorative letters*] | By | Sewell Stokes | With Illustrations by | GABRIEL ATKIN | [*epigraph*] | [*publisher's device*] | LONDON | The Richards Press Ltd. | PUBLISHERS

Crown 8°. $7\frac{1}{2}''$ × $4\frac{3}{4}''$. 248 pp. followed by 20-page publisher's catalogue inserted.

Issued in brown cloth boards. Lettered in black on upper cover: PILLORIED!; across spine: PILLORIED! | SEWELL | STOKES | RICHARDS. Printed on white laid paper with white laid endpapers. Top and fore edge trimmed; bottom edge rough trimmed. Heavy brown paper dust-jacket with black lettering and design by Gabriel Atkin, reproduced in line, within black diamond frame. The lower dust-jacket lists 'NEW & FORTHCOMING BOOKS' from Grant Richards, and the inside flap of the upper jacket shows the price, '7/6 NET'.

Published September 1928 at 7*s*. 6*d*.; the number of copies printed is not known.

The text of a postcard which Firbank sent from Rome to Sewell Stokes is quoted in the seventeenth essay, 'A Recent Genius' (pp. 219-30), on p. 223.

B2 RONALD FIRBANK A MEMOIR 1930

First edition:

RONALD FIRBANK | A MEMOIR BY IFAN KYRLE FLETCHER | WITH PERSONAL REMINISCENCES BY | LORD BERNERS, V. B. HOLLAND, | AUGUSTUS JOHN R.A., AND OSBERT SITWELL | [*black and white halftone portrait by Wyndham Lewis*] | WITH PORTRAITS BY | ALVARO GUEVARA, AUGUSTUS JOHN, R.A. | WYNDHAM LEWIS, AND CHARLES SHANNON, R.A. | DUCKWORTH | 3 HENRIETTA STREET, W. C. | 1930

Demy 8°. $8\frac{3}{4}''$ × $5\frac{1}{2}''$. 152 pp.

Issued in black cloth boards. Lettered in gilt on upper spine, upward: RONALD FIRBANK. Printed on white laid paper; white laid

B. CONTRIBUTIONS TO BOOKS AND PAMPHLETS

endpapers; top and fore edge trimmed, bottom edge rough trimmed. Cream white coated paper dust-jacket lettered in mauve and decorated with reproduction in mauve of a portrait drawing of Firbank by Augustus John within a five-rule frame. Lower dust-jacket announces the Rainbow Edition of Firbank's works (A12c) at 3s. 6d. a volume and a 'few copies' of 'ODETTE: A Fairy Tale for Weary People' (A4) as published in 1916 at 1s.

Published November 1930 at 8s. 6d.; probably 1,500 copies were printed.

Excerpts from Firbank's letters to de Vincheles Payen-Payne, Grant Richards, Carl Van Vechten, and C. R. W. Nevinson are printed for the first time as a part of Fletcher's 'A Memoir' (pp. 13-100); see pp. 25, 61, 81, 87, and 88.

B3   RONALD FIRBANK   1951

First edition:

RONALD FIRBANK | *by* | Jocelyn Brooke | LONDON | [*rule*] | ARTHUR BARKER LTD.
8°. 7¼" × 4¾". 104 pp.

Issued in red cloth boards with a rectangle, 1⅛" × 2", plate marked in black and lettered in red on upper cover: RONALD | FIRBANK; lettered in black across spine at head: [*double rule*] | RONALD | FIRBANK | [*five-point star*] | JOCELYN | BROOKE | [*five-point star*] | [*double rule*] and at tail: [*double rule*] | ARTHUR | BARKER | [*double rule*]. Printed on cream white wove paper; cream white wove endpapers. All edges trimmed. Grey and white coated paper dust-jacket lettered in bright blue and grey within white oval discs and, at centre, a drawing reproduced in grey within a white oval on the upper jacket; spine lettered in bright blue on white; lower jacket and both flaps have advertisements for previously published and forthcoming volumes in *The English Novelists* series.

Published June 1951 at 6s.; the number of copies printed is not known.

Numerous excerpts from Firbank's novels are quoted.

In January 1970, this book was reissued in 2,500 copies. None was available for examination.

B4   SOTHEBY & CO.'S CATALOGUE OF   1961
NINETEENTH-CENTURY & MODERN FIRST EDITIONS, PRESENTATION COPIES, AUTOGRAPH LETTERS & IMPORTANT LITERARY MANUSCRIPTS

B. CONTRIBUTIONS TO BOOKS AND PAMPHLETS

SOTHEBY & CO. | 34 & 35 NEW BOND STREET, LONDON, W. 1 [*on a plain panel*, $\frac{5}{8}''\times 3\frac{1}{16}''$, *within a quadruple-rule frame*] | CATALOGUE | OF | NINETEENTH-CENTURY & MODERN | FIRST EDITIONS, PRESENTATION COPIES, AUTOGRAPH LETTERS | & IMPORTANT LITERARY | MANUSCRIPTS | COMPRISING | *The Property of* DAME EDITH SITWELL, D.B.E., D.LITT. | *The Property of* THE LATE J. MIDDLETON MURRY, ESQ. | *The Property of* EVELYN WAUGH, ESQ. | *The Property of* RICHARD COBDEN-SANDERSON, ESQ. | *The Property of* MISS NANCY CUNARD | *The Property of* THE LATE SIR MAX BEERBOHM | *The Property of* LT.-COL. THOMAS FIRBANK, M.C. [*on a plain panel*, $3\frac{5}{16}''\times 3\frac{7}{8}''$, *within a quadruple-rule frame*] | Day of Sale: | TUESDAY, THE 12TH OF DECEMBER | AT ELEVEN O'CLOCK PRECISELY [*on a plain panel*, $1\frac{3}{16}''\times 3\frac{7}{8}''$, *within a quadruple-rule frame*] | 1961 [*on a plain panel*, $\frac{5}{16}''\times\frac{7}{8}''$, *within a curvilinear frame; all within a quadruple-rule frame, on a panel cross-hatched in black*] | Illustrated Catalogue (ten plates) 5s. 0d. [*on plain border*].

Royal 8°. $9\frac{5}{8}''\times 6\frac{1}{16}''$. 76 pp. with 10 plates tipped in.

Issued in green paper wrappers lettered in black. Upper wrapper serves as title-page. Lower wrapper, cross-hatched within frame identical with upper wrapper, indicates the history of Sotheby & Co. by designating on three plain panels, each $\frac{7}{8}''\times 2\frac{11}{16}''$, the names the firm has had since 1744. Wrappers are cut flush with edges; all edges trimmed. Printed on white wove paper; plates are on white wove paper heavier than text paper.

Published November 1961 at 5s.

Pp. [3]–21 offer for sale the 'manuscripts and correspondence of Ronald Firbank, including the autograph notebooks for all his major novels, the autograph MSS. of The New Rythum and a . . . series of 310 letters to his mother'. The descriptions, written by Mr Anthony Hobson, include quotations from the notebooks, other literary manuscripts, and the letters to Lady Firbank, all printed for the first time. Pp. 13 and 15 contain reproductions of drawings by Firbank within the text. Pages from Firbank's notebooks are reproduced, reduced, from line blocks on the verso of leaves (recto blank) facing pp. 5 and 13 and on the recto of leaves (verso blank) facing pp. 6 and 12. Part of a letter is reproduced on the recto of a leaf (verso blank) facing p. 18. Further excerpts, first printed, occur in the

B. CONTRIBUTIONS TO BOOKS AND PAMPHLETS

descriptions of letters addressed to Firbank and other miscellaneous materials, pp. 21-7.

A catalogue uniform in contents except that it lacks the plates was issued simultaneously in buff wrappers showing on the upper wrapper the price as 3d.

Text of pp. [3]-27 is reprinted without illustrations in *The New Rythum and Other Pieces* (A19) as an appendix (pp. 127-[35]).

B5 RONALD FIRBANK 1962

First edition:

RONALD FIRBANK | and | JOHN BETJEMAN | by JOCELYN BROOKE | PUBLISHED FOR | THE BRITISH COUNCIL | and the NATIONAL BOOK LEAGUE | by LONGMANS, GREEN & CO.

Demy 8°. $8\frac{1}{2}'' \times 5\frac{1}{2}''$. [ii], 48 pp.

Number 153 in the series, *Writers And Their Work*. Pp. 5-24 discuss Firbank.

Issued in chartreuse laid paper wrappers watermarked with a crown and the indecipherable name of a saint. Lettered in black and red on upper wrapper; the verso has brief statements about Firbank, John Betjeman, and Jocelyn Brooke. Lower wrapper, lettered in black, lists titles in the series *Writers And Their Work* on both verso and recto. Printed on cream laid paper. All edges trimmed. Wire stitched.

Published June 1962 at 2s. 6d.; the number of copies issued is not known.

Firbank's novels are quoted.

B6 A BIBLIOGRAPHY OF RONALD FIRBANK 1963

First edition:

A BIBLIOGRAPHY OF | RONALD FIRBANK | MIRIAM J. BENKOVITZ | RUPERT HART-DAVIS | SOHO SQUARE LONDON | 1963

Demy 8°. $8\frac{1}{4}'' \times 5\frac{7}{16}''$. vii, 103 pp., frontispiece and one illustration.

Issued in dark red cloth boards. Lettered in gilt across head of spine: SOHO | BIBLIO- | GRAPH- | IES | [*double rule*] | and across foot: RH-D; in centre of spine downward: Ronald Firbank MIRIAM BENKOVITZ. Printed on white wove paper, white wove endpapers. All edges trimmed; top edge stained dark red. Buff heavy wove paper

B. CONTRIBUTIONS TO BOOKS AND PAMPHLETS

dust-jacket lettered in black and red and decorated with publisher's device.

Published May 1963 at £2. 2s.; 1,063 copies were printed.

Excerpts from Firbank's letters to Lady Harriette Firbank, Heather Firbank, Grant Richards, Stuart Rose, and Carl Van Vechten are here printed for the first time. See pp. 17, 20, 23-4, 33, 35, 38, 39, 41, 45, 62, 70, 80, *et passim.*

B7   RONALD FIRBANK A BIOGRAPHY   1969

a. First edition:

RONALD | FIRBANK | [*decorative rule*] | *A Biography* | [*rule*] | MIRIAM J. BENKOVITZ | [*rule*] | [*publisher's device*] | ALFRED A. KNOPF | *New York* | 1969 [*within single-rule black frame*]

Demy 8°. $8\frac{5}{16}''$ × $5\frac{5}{8}''$. xviii, 300, xiv pp. and 12 pp. of illustrations. Issued in black cloth boards. Plate marked on upper cover: RONALD | FIRBANK | [*rule with loops at centre*]; lettered in gilt on spine downward: RONALD FIRBANK | [*rule with loops at both ends*] | *Miriam J. Benkovitz Alfred A. Knopf.* Printed on cream white wove paper; cream white wove endpapers. Top and bottom edges trimmed, top edge stained bright blue; fore edge rough trimmed. Buff and black wove paper dust-jacket lettered in bright blue, white, and buff and decorated with half-tone reproduction in black on buff of portrait-drawing of Firbank by Augustus John.

Published May 1969 at $6.95; 4,000 copies were printed.

The fragments 'Lay of the Last Nurserymaid' (Ms 3) and ['Lila'] (Ms 4) are printed in their entirety for the first time. See pp. 20, 16-17. Excerpts from Firbank's letters to Lady Harriette Firbank, Heather Firbank, Grant Richards, Stuart Rose, Ragland Somerset, and Carl Van Vechten are here printed for the first time. See pp. 103, 111, 128, 133, 149, 161, 187, 209, 214, 227, 228, 234, 237, 246, 263, 279, 287, 289, 290 *et passim.*

b. First edition, English issue (1970):

RONALD | FIRBANK | *A Biography* | MIRIAM J. BEN-KOVITZ | WEIDENFELD AND NICOLSON | 5 Winsley Street London W 1

The English issue, $8\frac{1}{2}''$ × $5\frac{1}{4}''$, was produced by photolithography and is uniform with American issue except for altered title page;

B. CONTRIBUTIONS TO BOOKS AND PAMPHLETS

imprint, p. [iv]; and lack of two printer's leaves, note on the author, and colophon (pp. [xi and xiii], American issue). Twelve pages of illustrations produced in half-tone on cream white coated paper are sewn between pp. 172 and 173 in the American issue and between pp. 158 and 159 in the English. Issued in black cloth boards lettered in gilt across the spine: Miriam J. | Benkovitz | [*printer's device*] | *Ronald* | *Firbank* | Weidenfeld | & Nicolson. All edges trimmed; bottom edge stained orange. Printed on cream white wove paper; cream white wove endpapers. White and orange coated paper dust-jacket lettered in black with a portrait of Firbank by Augustus John reproduced in half-tone within an elaborate fuchsia and purple frame. Published January 1970 at 63s. or £3.15.

B8   RONALD FIRBANK   1969

First edition:

RONALD FIRBANK | [*four inch rule*] | By JAMES DOUGLAS MERRITT | *Brooklyn College, City University of New York* | [*publisher's device*] | Twayne Publishers, Inc. :: New York

Demy 8°. 8" × 5¼". 152 pp.

Issued in dark red leatherette boards. Blocked in silver on upper cover: Ronald Firbank | James Douglas Merritt | [*publisher's device*]; across spine at head: TEAS | [*publisher's device*] | [*rule*] | 93 | [*rule*] and at tail: [*rule*] | TWAYNE; at centre of spine, downward: Ronald Firbank [*horizontal rule*] James Douglas | Merritt. Printed on cream white wove paper; dark red wove endpapers of heavier stock. All edges trimmed. Probably issued without dust-jacket.

Published as Number 93 in Twayne's *English Authors* Series late in 1969 at $4.50; 2,000 copies were printed.

Firbank's novels and notebooks are quoted.

B9   RONALD FIRBANK   [1970]

First edition:

RONALD FIRBANK | by EDWARD MARTIN POTOKER | [*publisher's device*] | *Columbia University Press* | NEW YORK & LONDON 1969

Crown 8°. 8" × 5½". 48 pp.

Issued in white glazed stiff paper wrappers lettered in orange and black on upper wrapper: Columbia Essays on Modern Writers

B. CONTRIBUTIONS TO BOOKS AND PAMPHLETS

43/$1.00 | Ronald Firbank | Edward Martin Potoker | [*four-inch rule*] | [*large black and white geometric design*]. Lower wrapper lists the editional board of the Columbia Essays on Modern Writers, forty-six essays, and their authors. Printed on cream white wove paper. All edges trimmed. Wire stitched.

Published in 1970, probably in late February, at $1; 7,500 copies were printed.

Firbank's novels are quoted extensively. See pp. 7-8, 10, 13, 18, 27, 29, 30, 33-4, 35, 40, 41, 45 *et passim*.

B10   PRANCING NOVELIST   1973

First edition:

PRANCING NOVELIST | A DEFENCE OF FICTION | IN THE FORM OF A | CRITICAL BIOGRAPHY | IN PRAISE OF | RONALD FIRBANK | BY | BRIGID BROPHY | MACMILLAN

16mo. $9\frac{1}{2}'' \times 6''$. xvi, 592 pp., and 8 pp. of illustrations.

Issued in maroon cloth boards. Lettered in silver across head of spine within grey panel with single-rule silver frame, $1\frac{11}{16}'' \times 1\frac{1}{2}''$: PRANCING | NOVELIST | Brigid | Brophy; and at foot: MACMILLAN. Printed on white wove paper; white wove endpapers of heavier stock; illustrations on white coated paper. All edges trimmed. White and pale green coated paper dust-jacket with upper jacket lettered in orange and white; spine lettered in orange and black; on lower jacket is a black and white photograph of Brigid Brophy with information about her. Inner flaps have information about the book, credits for the cover, SBN 333 13779 5, and price.

Published March 1973 at £8.00; the number of copies printed is not available.

Firbank's letters and fiction are quoted.

B11   RONALD FIRBANK MEMOIRS AND   1977
             CRITIQUES

First edition:

RONALD FIRBANK | MEMOIRS AND CRITIQUES | edited with an introduction by | MERVYN HORDER | [*publisher's device*] | DUCKWORTH

Demy 8°. $8\frac{1}{2}'' \times 5\frac{1}{4}''$. xii, 228 pp.

B. CONTRIBUTIONS TO BOOKS AND PAMPHLETS

Issued in black cloth boards. Lettered in gilt on spine downward: Ronald Firbank Memoirs and Critiques Edited by Mervyn Horder Duckworth. Printed on cream white wove paper; white wove endpapers. All edges trimmed. Purple coated paper dust-jacket lettered in white and decorated with a portrait of Firbank by Augustus John reproduced in grey within a single-rule black frame. The lower jacket lists Duckworth publications and the inner flaps advertise this book and other books by Firbank.

Published late in 1977 at £5.95; 4,750 copies were issued.

Occasional excerpts from Firbank's novels and excerpts from his letters as first printed in *Ronald Firbank A Memoir* by Ifan Kyrle Fletcher (B2) are quoted.

C.
CONTRIBUTIONS TO PERIODICALS

C1   LA PRINCESSE AUX SOLEILS ROMANCE PARLÉE
        "Les Essais." Revue Mensuelle, II (November 1904), 78–80.
        Signed: Arthur Firbank. Below the signature is: (*Trad. de l'anglais par l'auteur*). Firbank's first publication. Reprinted with an English version by Edgell Rickword in *La Princesse aux Soleils & Harmonie*, pp. 1–2 (A27).

C2   HARMONIE
        "Les Essais." Revue Mensuelle, II (February 1905), 305–6.
        Signed: Arthur Firbank. Below the signature is: (*Trad. de l'anglais par l'auteur*). Reprinted with an English version by Edgell Rickword in *La Princesse aux Soleils & Harmonie*, p. 9 (A27).

C3   SOUVENIR D'AUTOMNE. A POEM IN PROSE
        Supplement to *The King and His Navy and Army*, XXI (2 December 1905), 11.
        Signed: Arthur Annesley Ronald Firbank. Excerpt reprinted with the original title 'Impression d'Automne — A Poem in Prose' in *The New Rythum*, p. 116 (A19; cf. Ts 4).

C4   "THE WAVERING DISCIPLE." A FANTASIA
        The Granta, XX (24 November 1906), 110–11.
        Signed: A. A. R. Firbank. Consists of Parts I and II. Reprinted in *Granta 75*, pp. 19–20 (C11), and *Two Early Stories*, pp. [13]–19 (A26).

C5   [Ibid.]
        The Granta, XX (5 December 1906), 130–2.
        Signed: A. A. R. Firbank. Consists of Part III. Reprinted in *Granta 75*, pp. 20–1 (C11), and *Two Early Stories*, pp. [20]–7 (A26).

C5.1   AN EARLY FLEMISH PAINTER
        The Academy, LXXIII (28 September 1903), 948.
        Signed: Arthur Firbank. Reprinted separately (A24).

C6   A STUDY IN OPAL
        The Granta, XXI (2 November 1907), 54–60.
        Signed: A. A. F. Firbank identified 'A Study in Opal' as an early work in a letter to Carl Van Vechten dated 22 June 1925. Reprinted in *Two Early Stories*, pp. [31]–54 (A26).

C7   FANTASIA FOR ORCHESTRA IN F SHARP MINOR
        Art and Letters, II N.S. (Spring 1919), 64–79 (pp. 67 and 73 contain drawings unrelated to the text; pp. 68 and 74 are blank).
        Signed: Ronald Firbank. According to Osbert Sitwell, Firbank read 'Fantasia' aloud after a dinner party given in his honour at the Golden Cross Inn, Oxford, in February 1919. Sitwell arranged for subsequent publication (*Noble Essences*,

C. CONTRIBUTIONS TO PERIODICALS

pp. 74-6). Reprinted with extensive revision as the eighth chapter of *Valmouth*, pp. 127-56 (A6a).

C8   A BROKEN ORCHID (FROM SORROW IN SUNLIGHT)
The Reviewer, IV (October 1923), 15-19.
Signed: Ronald Firbank. Firbank's first publication in America.

In November 1922 Firbank, then in Bordighera, received a copy of *The Reviewer*; Carl Van Vechten had sent it with the request that Firbank submit a short piece for publication. He acknowledged the periodical in a letter of 2 December and added that he 'should love' to write for it, but his description of possible contributions was sheer nonsense: a 'little thing called "Filtered Water" ' much too pure to send, an ' "all British" musical comedy' with a 'divine libretto (panting for music)', a 'Prose-poem on "Violets", dealing, as they say, with those of Oxford, Naples, & Athens — not to forget *Parma*'. He wrote again on 20 March 1923 to say that he seemed to manage nothing to his liking, though he had recently started a 'conte called "The Story of Percy Eton & Evie Cutbush", but "Evie" grew too terrible & Percy took to his heels'. He could not resist Van Vechten indefinitely, however; in a letter dated 23 April 1923, after saying he felt 'quite guilty' about *The Reviewer*, Firbank offered to send the ' "Earthquake" chapter' from his new novel. He did so on 16 July 1923.

Reprinted with some revision as the eleventh chapter of *Prancing Nigger*, pp. 81-9 (A10a).

C9   LADY APPLEDORE'S MÉSALLIANCE
Cornhill Magazine, CLXXII (Summer, 1962), [399]-425.
Signed: Arthur Annesley Ronald Firbank. Reprinted in *The New Rythum and Other Pieces*, pp. [31]-67 (A19).

C10 THE NEW RYTHUM
Portfolio, No. 7 (Winter 1963), 57, 59-63, 99-108.
Signed: Ronald Firbank. P. 57 is a fly-title with an illustration by Larry Rivers; p. 63 has a second illustration. Pp. 56, 58, 112-14 contain an introduction and on pp. 56 and 58 are reproductions of photographs illustrative of Firbank's environment and work. The text is that of the bound notebook (Ms 6b) and uniform with the text of *The New Rythum and Other Pieces*, pp. [69]-107 (A19a).

C11 THE WAVERING DISCIPLE
Granta 75, LXVIII (15 February 1964), 19-21.
Signed: Ronald Firbank. The text is that of the first publication in *The Granta*, 24 November and 5 December 1906, pp. 110-11 and 130-2 (C4 and C5). Reprinted in *Two Early Stories*, pp. [13]-27 (A26).

MANUSCRIPTS AND TYPESCRIPTS

Although few of Firbank's published works exist in manuscript or typescript, a considerable number of his papers survive, preserved mostly by Lady Firbank and, after her death, by Ronald and then by his sister Heather. Apart from letters and miscellaneous documents — reading lists, lists of friends to whom he wanted Richards to send gift copies of novels, excerpts from reviews, and a French exercise book — the papers consist of literary manuscripts and typescripts and an important set of holograph notebooks. Most were a part of the Firbank family papers. On 12 December 1961 Messrs Sotheby sold these at auction. All items inspected while still in the possession of the family are designated by an FP; when they are known, the names of persons or institutions who acquired manuscripts and typescripts as a result of the sale are appended. Similarly, names of those who own manuscripts and typescripts which were not involved in the Sotheby sale are also given. Because the exact date of several manuscripts and still more typescripts cannot be determined, these are put in alphabetical order.

I. MANUSCRIPTS

Ms 1   "FAR AWAY"
Four leaves of The Coopers, Chislehurst letter paper; dated 'Paris, 24 July 1904'. Published separately (A22).
(FP; Miriam J. Benkovitz)

Ms 2   IDEAS AND FANCIES
Ten leaves interleaved with eight gold gauze leaves. Signed 'Arthur Firbank'. In white paper wrappers lettered and decorated with water-colours by Firbank. Inside the upper wrapper he wrote, 'For darling Baba [his mother] from Artie with much love for Christmas 1904 —.' Contents include text published as 'Harmonie' (C2, A27) on seventh (verso blank) and eighth leaves and text of ' "The Lieutenant & the Irise's Wife" a Parable' on tenth leaf and inside lower wrapper preceded by nine water-colours.
(FP; Lord Horder)

Ms 3   LAY OF THE LAST NURSERYMAID
One leaf of lined paper, verso blank, torn from a notebook. Poem of ten lines. Below the title Firbank wrote, '(Keep)'. Published in *Ronald Firbank A Biography*, p. 20 (B7).
(FP; Miriam J. Benkovitz)

Ms 4   [LILA]
One leaf torn from a notebook. Fragment of a novel which Firbank wrote at the age of ten; he described it in a letter of

MANUSCRIPTS AND TYPESCRIPTS

22 June 1925 to Carl Van Vechten as similar to *Young Visiters*. Excerpt published in *The New Rythum*, p. 115 (A19). Entire fragment published in *Ronald Firbank A Biography*, pp. 16-17 (B7).

(FP; Miriam J. Benkovitz)

Ms   "MR. WHITE-MORGAN THE DIAMOND KING"
a. Six leaves of The Coopers, Chislehurst letter paper. Excerpt published in *The New Rythum*, p. 115.

(FP)

b. Two leaves, integral.

(Berg Collection)

Ms 6   " 'THE NEW RYTHUM' "
a. Sixty-two leaves, versos blank, including four leaves of notes. Rough draft, revised throughout, of seven chapters of the incomplete novel later entitled *The New Rythum*.

(FP; Mrs A. McNeill Donohue; Columbia University)

b. Fifty-four leaves, versos blank, of a bound notebook of 80 leaves. Fair copy signed 'Ronald Firbank'. Published in *The New Rythum and Other Pieces*, pp. [69]-107 (A19a-b) and in *Portfolio*, Winter, 1963, pp. 57, 59-63, 99-108 (C10).

(FP; Mrs A. McNeill Donohue; Columbia University)

c. Scraps of two leaves, carelessly torn, versos blank. Rough notes.

(Berg Collection)

Ms 7   [Preface for the American edition of *The Flower Beneath the Foot*]
a. Four leaves, versos blank. Rough draft, revised throughout.

(FP; Mrs A. McNeill Donohue; Columbia University)

b. Three leaves, versos blank. Fair copy, as published, pp. [v-vii] (A9b), but lacking signature.

(Stuart Rose)

Ms 8   LA PRINCESSE AUX SOLEILS (ROMANCE PARLÉE)
a. Ten leaves. Signed 'Arthur Firbank'. French text followed by English text with water-colour decorations throughout. On p. [1] Firbank wrote, 'Written and painted by Artie to Darling Baba with much love for her birthday 1904.' White paper wrappers decorated with water-colours.

(FP)

b. Seven leaves of which one has verso blank. Signed 'Arthur Firbank'. White paper wrappers decorated with water-colours. Inside upper wrapper Firbank wrote, 'A ma soeur adorée j'envoie la deuxième edition de mon livre — Artie 5 Septembre 1904.' Published in *"Les Essais,"* November 1904, pp. 78-80 (C1); reprinted with an English version by Edgell Rickword in *La Princesse aux Soleils & Harmonie*, pp. 1-2 (A27).

(FP; Anthony d'Offay)

MANUSCRIPTS AND TYPESCRIPTS

Ms 9   REVERIE AND FLAVIA
Nine leaves of a bound notebook of 113 leaves. Two essays in French.
(FP; Fales Collection)

Ms 10   ['The Roses were never called ...']
Five leaves, versos blank.
(FP; Humanities Research Center, The University of Texas)

Ms 11   SANTAL
Not available for inspection. Probably the manuscript described in a catalogue issued by Messrs Frank Hollings (once of 45 Cloth Fair, London, EC1) as consisting of thirty-five leaves 'written in violet ink on one side' in a folio notebook. The manuscript so described, Firbank gave to Helen Carewe, the Ἑλένη of the *Santal* dedication. (A8a).
(Thomas Horan)

Ms 12   [Six miscellaneous fragments including one leaf beginning 'If Julia...' and dated '24.4.25'.]
(FP; Fales Collection)

Ms 13   "THE WIND & THE ROSES"
Two leaves, versos blank. Signed 'Arthur Firbank'. Published separately (A21).
(FP; Alan Clodd)

II. NOTEBOOKS

Ms 14   One notebook, 60 leaves, with miscellaneous notes for *The Artificial Princess* (A13a), *Vainglory* (A2a), and *The Princess Zoubaroff* (A7).
(FP; Mrs A. McNeill Donohue; Columbia University)

Ms 15   Fifteen notebooks, 803 leaves, for *Vainglory* (A2a).
(FP; Mrs A. McNeill Donohue; Columbia University)

Ms 16   Ten notebooks, 591 leaves, for *Inclinations* (A3).
(FP; Fales Collection)

Ms 17   Four notebooks, 310 leaves, for *Caprice* (A5) of which two contain some notes for *Valmouth* (A6a).
(FP; Houghton Library, Harvard University)

Ms 18   Eight notebooks, 448 leaves, for *Valmouth* (A6a) of which one contains some notes for *The Princess Zoubaroff* (A7). That one notebook, 47 leaves, is a part of the Berg Collection. The other seven, once among the Firbank papers, are now at the Humanities Research Center, the University of Texas.

Ms 19   Two notebooks, 121 leaves, for *The Princess Zoubaroff* (A7).
(FP; Anthony d'Offay; Miriam J. Benkovitz)

MANUSCRIPTS AND TYPESCRIPTS

Ms 20 Two notebooks, 43 leaves, with 10 leaves laid in one book of 3 leaves, for *Santal* (A8a; Ms 11). One (40 leaves) was once among the Firbank papers.
(Berg Collection)

Ms 21 Five notebooks, 230 leaves, for *The Flower Beneath the Foot* (A9a) of which one contains some notes for *Santal* (A8a).
(FP; Jack H. Samuels; Columbia University)

Ms 22 Four notebooks, 118 leaves, for *Prancing Nigger* (A10a); one of these (16 leaves) is a part of the Berg Collection. The other three, formerly among the Firbank papers and then the property of Mrs A. McNeill Donohue, are now a part of the Rare Book and Manuscript Library, Columbia University.

Ms 23 Four notebooks, 258 leaves, for *Concerning the Eccentricities of Cardinal Pirelli* (A11) of which one contains some notes for *The New Rythum* (A19; C10; Ms 6a). Excerpts published in *The New Rythum*, pp. 108-12.
(FP; Berg Collection)

Ms 24 Two notebooks, 178 leaves, with 5 leaves laid in one book, for *The New Rythum* (A19; C10).
(FP; Mrs A. McNeill Donohue; Columbia University)

III. TYPESCRIPTS

Ts 1 THE ARTIFICIAL PRINCESS
a. Thirty-eight leaves, versos blank, containing the first two chapters, with holograph revisions throughout. The title, p. [1], has been altered from 'SALOME, OR 'TIS A PITY THAT SHE WOULD'. Dark green paper wrappers. Across the top left corner of the upper wrapper is written in an unidentified hand, 'Mr Firbank 87 Brook Street calling July 1st double spacing. Friday morn. No Binding.' Laid in are two leaves (versos blank), one containing holograph notes for a foreword, text, and title; the other a holograph draft of an incomplete foreword.
(Berg Collection)

b. Thirty-one leaves, versos blank, containing an incomplete third chapter ending with ' "A merciful end" , the Baroness bewilderedly told herself.'; holograph revisions throughout. On the verso of the last leaf is the stamp of Ethel Christian's Typewriting Office. Dark green paper wrappers. Laid in are four leaves, versos blank, with the remainder of the text, as printed, in Firbank's hand. (Cf. p. 48.)
(Berg Collection)

c. Eighty-two leaves, versos blank, containing an incomplete text as described above; holograph revisions throughout. At the foot of the last leaf and on its verso Firbank completed the text, writing in purple ink. Brick-red paper wrappers. In-

MANUSCRIPTS AND TYPESCRIPTS

side the upper wrapper, the author wrote his name and this address, 'Villa Primrose, Boulevard de la Plage, Arcachon, Gironde, France.'

(Berg Collection)

d. Eighty-three leaves, versos blank, containing fair copy of complete text. Grey paper wrappers. (A13a).

(FP; Berg Collection)

Ts 1.1 CONCERNING THE ECCENTRICITIES OF CARDINAL PIRELLI
Ninety-two leaves, versos blank, containing fair copy of complete text (A11) with occasional autograph corrections. Signed 'Ronald Firbank'. Grey paper wrappers with blue paper label pasted on upper cover. On the label is typed: ⁂ | CONCERNING | THE | ECCENTRICITIES | OF | CARDINAL | PIRELLI | ⁂

(Berg Collection)

Ts 2 A DISCIPLE FROM THE COUNTRY
Thirty-five leaves, versos blank. On first leaf, p. [1], is a holograph note, *'Not to be published'*. Lacks title-leaf and upper wrapper; lower wrapper is blue-grey paper. Excerpt published in *The New Rythum*, pp. 120-[8] (A19).

(FP; Mrs A. McNeill Donohue; Columbia University)

Ts 2.1 "FAR AWAY"
Three leaves, versos blank, and one blank leaf. Signed: 'Arthur Firbank'. A fair copy of the manuscript text of 1904 (Ms 1) with minor textual changes; lacks 'Paris, 24 July 1904'. Green paper wrappers.

(Miriam J. Benkovitz)

Ts 3 "HER DEAREST FRIEND"
Nine leaves, versos blank. Signed 'ARTHUR FIRBANK'. On title-leaf, p. [i], is a holograph note, 'Not to be published'; on first page of text, p. 1, is holograph correction. Green paper wrappers.

(FP; Miriam J. Benkovitz)

Ts 4 IMPRESSION D'AUTOMNE. – A POEM IN PROSE
Three leaves, versos blank. Signed 'Arthur Annesley Ronald Firbank'; dated 'Oct. 7th 1905'. Dark green paper wrappers. Published as 'Souvenir d'Automne' (C3); excerpt published in *The New Rythum*, p. 116 (A19).

(FP; Miriam J. Benkovitz)

Ts 5 INCLINATIONS. CHAPTER IV. PART II
Eleven leaves, versos blank, containing the revised dinner party chapter printed first in *The Works of Ronald Firbank*, Vol. II, pp. 133-41 (A12a). Dated 'Rome April 1925'.

(FP; Claude Smith Jr.)

MANUSCRIPTS AND TYPESCRIPTS

Ts 6   "LADY APPLEDORE'S MESALLIANCE" (AN ARTIFICIAL PASTORAL)
Forty-one leaves, versos blank. Signed 'A. A. R. Firbank'. On title-leaf, p. [i], is holograph note, '? Revise considerably in places — If —'. A final blank leaf (not included in count) bears the stamp of a Cambridge typing bureau. Green paper wrappers. Published in *Cornhill Magazine*, Summer, 1962, pp. [399]-425 (C9); reprinted in *The New Rythum and Other Pieces*, pp. [31]-67 (A19).
(FP; Miriam J. Benkovitz)

Ts 7   THE LEGEND OF SAINT GABRIELLE
Five leaves, versos blank. Signed 'ARTHUR FIRBANK'. On title-leaf, p. [i], is holograph note, 'Not to be published. RF.'; on last leaf is holograph revision. Dark green paper wrappers.
(FP; Miriam J. Benkovitz)

Ts 8   "THE MAUVE TOWER"
a. Twenty-seven leaves, versos blank. Signed 'ARTHUR FIRBANK'. On title-leaf, p. [i], is holograph note, 'Not to publish!'; on the second leaf, p. [ii], is this dedication, 'A Monsieur Jean Pozzi tres cordialement je dédie ma "Tour Mauve" en souvenir de l'été mil neuf cent quatre.' Dark green paper wrappers. Excerpt published in *The New Rythum*, pp. 117-18 (A19).
(FP; Rochester University Library)

b. A second typescript uniform with the first with additional blank leaf; lacks holograph note.
(Miriam J. Benkovitz)

Ts 9   ODETTE D'ANTREVERNES A FAIRY TALE FOR WEARY PEOPLE
Thirteen leaves, versos blank. Signed 'ARTHUR FIRBANK'. A fair copy of the 1905 text (A1a). Dark green paper wrappers.
(FP; M. H. Mushlin)

Ts 10   THE SINGING BIRD & THE MOON
Nine leaves, versos blank. Signed 'Arthur Annesley Ronald Firbank'. On title-leaf, p. [i], is holograph note, 'Not to be published RF —'. Green paper wrappers.
(FP; Rochester University Library)

Ts 11   A TRAGEDY IN GREEN
Nineteen leaves, versos blank. On first leaf, p. [1], is dedication, 'To The Inspirer of the Tragedy, Sir Coleridge Kennard. —' and holograph note, 'Not to be published RF.' Some holograph revisions throughout. Dark green paper wrappers. Excerpt published in *The New Rythum*, pp. 118-19 (A19).

MANUSCRIPTS AND TYPESCRIPTS

Published complete in *When Widows Love & A Tragedy in Green*, pp. 25-36 (A29).

(FP; Fales Collection)

Ts 12 "TRUE LOVE"
a. Ten leaves, versos blank. Signed 'ARTHUR FIRBANK'. On the title-leaf, p. [i], is holograph note, 'Not to publish RF.' Green paper wrappers. Excerpt published in *The New Rythum*, p. 119 (A19).

(FP; Rochester University Library)

b. Typescript uniform with the above. Lacks holograph note.

(FP; Miriam J. Benkovitz)

Ts 13 "WHEN WIDOWS LOVE"
Eleven leaves, versos blank. Signed 'ARTHUR FIRBANK'. On title-leaf, p. [i], is holograph note, 'Not to be published *RF*.' Dark grey paper wrappers. Excerpt published as 'The Widow's Love' in *The New Rythum*, pp. 116-17 (A19). Published complete in *When Widows Love & A Tragedy in Green*, pp. [15]-24 (A29).

(FP; Fales Collection)

APPENDIX:
SUPPOSITITIOUS WORKS

Ronald Firbank's authorship of any printed item not already recorded is open to question. Two, however, claim consideration, the first because there is reason to think it is his and the second because it is usually attributed to Firbank.

THE FAIRIES WOOD [n.d.]

'The Fairies Wood' is a poem of five rhyming quatrains printed on one side of a heavy white card $4\frac{1}{2}'' \times 3\frac{1}{2}''$, all edges gilt, and signed 'A. F.'.

Apart from the signature, the evidence that Firbank is the author, flimsy as it may be, is this letter to his mother dated 30 October 1898:

> I hope you will like this piece of poetary I have written for you. It is not much but I should like you to have it only dont show it any boday else I made it up all myself & as Joey [Ronald's older brother] would say 'did not look in a fairy book for it,' be sure not to show it anybody.

That Lady Firbank, with characteristic devotion and pride in her son's gifts, disregarded his instructions and had the poem printed can be only conjecture. The number of copies printed is unknown; very likely the card was not offered for sale. The only copy available for inspection was among the Firbank papers. It is presently in the private collection of Anthony d'Offay.

COUNT FANNY'S NUPTIALS 1907

Count Fanny's | Nuptials: | Being | The Story of a Courtship | BY | SIMON ARROW | *Printed for private circulation, and published by* | G. G. HOPE JOHNSTONE.

Royal 8°. $10'' \times 7\frac{1}{2}''$. 72 pp. and 7 illustrations.

P. [1] half-title; p. [2] blank; p. [3] title; p. [4] blank; p. [5] dedication, 'To | CLARENCE. | [rule] | *"Quod habuit haec fecit — he has done what | he could."* | [rule] | With what a chastened spirit you have | always approached such nice matters as the | knotting of a scarf — the conduct of a cane! | With what a wealth of imagination you | have always selected your flower. | Soon we shall have our young men | wearing patches — a pretty protest, say I, | against the degradation of Fashion.'; p. [6] blank; pp. 7-[69] text; pp. [70-2] blank. Illustrations, black and white line cuts within a wide single-rule frame on white coated paper, tipped in facing pp. 16, 20, 30, 44, 46, 50, and 58. Issued in dark blue cloth boards with bevelled edges. Lettered in gilt across spine: COUNT | FANNY'S | NUPTIALS | BY | SIMON | ARROW | 1907.

Printed on cream white laid paper; cream white laid endpapers. All edges rough trimmed. No dust-jacket available.

APPENDIX: SUPPOSITITIOUS WORKS

Details of publication are unknown.

Attribution of the book to Firbank rests on hearsay. Booksellers have confirmed the fact that on the basis of a superficial resemblance of the text to Firbank's work, they identified Simon Arrow as Ronald Firbank some time after the book appeared. Over the years the attribution stuck for lack of evidence to the contrary. Then in his discussion of the illustrations as Beardsley forgeries, R. A. Walker named Firbank as the author of *Count Fanny's Nuptials* (*How to Detect Beardsley Forgeries*, Bedford, 1950, p. 24). But in a letter dated 20 July 1960 Walker wrote that he had no justification for his statement about Firbank, that he merely accepted the usual attribution as the correct one.

Certainly no facts support Firbank's authorship. In the years just before 1907, when he had a childish readiness to see his writing in print, Firbank appears to have been fully occupied with other publications and possibly an unpublished work. (Cf. A1a, C1-6, Ts 8.) His letters refer often to his writing, published or not; *Count Fanny's Nuptials* is never mentioned. Prurience was no deterrent to Firbank's acknowledging authorship. Firbank took for granted that the unconventional character of his books was often shocking, and, as he said in a letter to Van Vechten, he was 'dead and indifferent' to comments on his 'supposed wickedness'.

On the other hand, there is no proof that Firbank is not the author. That must depend on either a positive identification of Simon Arrow or a careful textual analysis.

The British Library takes no note of the attribution to Firbank.

ACKNOWLEDGMENTS

To do more than recognize, in the space at my disposal, the great variety of assistance I have received with this book is impossible. Fully aware of its inadequacy as a measure of my indebtedness, I can only make a list in alphabetical order of the individuals and institutions who helped me assemble this account of Ronald Firbank's literary life:

Mr Alan Anderson; Mr Gene Andrewski; Dr Middendorf of the Bayerische Staatsbibliothek, Munchen; Mr John D. Gordan, Curator, Miss Beatrice Landskronner, and Mrs Charles Szladits of the Henry W. and Albert A. Berg Collection (The New York Public Library); Casa Editrice Valentino Bompiani & C., Milano; Booth American Shipping Corporation; Mr Charles Brackett; Mr Neville Braybrooke; British Museum; Mr Richard Buckle; Cambridge University Library; Mr Roderick Cave; Centro Nazionale Di Informazioni Bibliografiche, Roma; Mrs Clarice J. Alston, Librarian of *Chicago Daily Defender*; Library of Congress; Mrs Lloyd Lemons of Coward-McCann, Inc.; Miss Nancy Cunard; Baker Library of Dartmouth College; Mr Eric J. Dingwall; Colonel Marston E. Drake of James F. Drake, Inc.; Dramatists Guild; Miss Emily Driscoll; Lord Horder, Miss Sandra Soames, and Mr Charles Walton of Gerald Duckworth & Co., Ltd.; Mr Vernon Duke; Mr Hugh Easton; Mr Richard G. Medley and his staff member Mr W. A. Brown of Field Roscoe & Co.; Mr Lew David Feldman; Colonel L. T. Firbank; Colonel Thomas Firbank; Mr Ifan Kyrle Fletcher; Mr Edwin Gilcher; Miss Alice Goodman; Grove Press, Inc.; Professor Bruce Harkness; Mr Rupert Hart-Davis and staff of Rupert Hart-Davis Ltd.; Professor Edith F. Hayter; Mr John Hayward; Professor John P. Heins; Mr A. R. A. Hobson; Mr A. T. Miller of Frank Hollings; Professor Julia H. Hysham; Library of the

ACKNOWLEDGMENTS

University of Illinois; Mr Philip Kaplan; Mr Fenton Keyes; Mr Jean Lambert; Mr Dan H. Laurence; Mr Max Niedermayer of Limes Verlag, Wiesbaden; Lloyd's Register of Shipping; Mr David Conyers of London Management & Representation Ltd.; Mr Samuel Loveman; Miss L. Marion Moshier; Mr A. N. L. Munby; Miss May Davenport Seymour, Curator of the Theatre and Music Collection, Museum of the City of New York; Miss Winifred A. Myers; Mr F. S. Parker of Nashville Trust Co.; Mr Edwin V. Erbe and Mr Robert M. MacGregor of New Directions; *New York Herald Tribune*; The New York Public Library; New York State Library; Mr Anthony d'Offay; Dr K. Kuczewski of the Österreichische Nationalbibliothek, Wien; Penguin Books Ltd.; Phoenix Book Shop; Mr Thomas Rae; Professor John K. Reeves; Mr Stuart Rose; Mr Anthony Rota; Mr Bertram Rota; Mr Martin Secker; Mr Brian Sewell; Mr George F. Sims; Miss Gladys M. Brownell, Librarian, and Miss Jane G. Rollins of Skidmore College Library; Miss M. Elizabeth Barber and staff of the Society of Authors; Sotheby & Co.; Professor Esther L. Stallman; Stechert-Hafner, Inc.; Mr Arthur J. H. Sudbury; Mr Frank Sullivan; Mr Alan G. Thomas; Mr Virgil Thomson; Mr Timothy d'Arch Smith of The Times Bookshop; The *Times Literary Supplement*; Union College Library; Mr Theodore G. Hartry of the United States Information Agency; Mr Joseph Scott, Librarian, Mr Douglas G. F. Walker, Deputy Librarian, and Mr Ian Angus of The Library of University College London; Mr Dan Totheroh; Professor Dorothy W. Upton; Mr Carl Van Vechten; Mr Peter K. Thornton, Assistant Keeper, and Miss Madelaine Blumstein of the Department of Textiles, Victoria and Albert Museum; Mr Arthur Waley; Professor Donald C. Gallup, Mr Donald G. Wing, and Miss Marjorie G. Wynne of Yale University Library; Mr R. A. Walker; A. P. Watt & Son; Professor Mary Elizabeth Williams; Mr Sandy Wilson; Mr Cecil Woolf.

INDEX

Main references are shown in heavy type. The letters Ap refer to the Appendix.

Aberdeen, Lord A7
Academy, The A24; C5.1
Alaistair (Hans Henning Voight) A4
Albani, Dame Emma, *see Letter from Arthur Ronald Firbank to Madam Albani, A*
Albondocani Press (New York) A26
Alexandra, Queen A1b
Andrewski (Gene) and Associates A6a
Arrow, Simon Ap
Art and Letters (New York) C7
Artificial Princess, The A12a, c, d, f, 13a-b, 15, 16, 17a; Ms 14; Ts 1a-d; *see also* Extravaganzas; *Princesse Artificielle suivi de Mon Piaffeur Noir, La*
Associated Negro Press A10a
Atkin, Gabriel B1
Author Hunting (Richards) A10a

Baba A2a, 5; Ms 2, 8a; *see also* Firbank, Lady Harriette Jane Garrett
Barker (Arthur) Ltd. (London) B3
Baylis (Ebenezer) and Son Ltd. (Worcester) A19a
Beardsley, Aubrey A2a
Beerbohm, Sir Max B4
Benkovitz, Miriam J. A20, 21, 22, 24, 26, 27; B6, 7a-b; Ms 3, 4; Ts 2.1, 3, 6, 7, 8b, 12b
Berg Collection, Henry W. and Albert A. (The New York Public Library) A1b, 4; Ms 5b, 6c, 20, 22, 23; Ts 1a-d; Ts 1.1
Berners, Lord A2a; B2
Betjeman, John B5
'Bibliography of the First Editions of Books by Arthur Annesley Ronald Firbank (1886-1926), A' (Muir) A1b, 10b
Bibliography of Ronald Firbank, A (Benkovitz), B6
Bicker's & Son (London) A1b
Billing and Sons Ltd. (Guildford) A12d

'Biographical Memoir' (Sitwell) A12a
Bompiani S. A. — Editrice (Rome) A16
Bonacio & Saul (New York) A8b
Boni, Albert and Charles (New York) A9b
Book of Scoundrels (Whibley) A9a
Bookman's Journal (London), Supplement to A1b
Bookseller, The (London) A5, 12d, 13a
Boston Evening Transcript A10a, 15
Bradley, William A. A16
Brady, William A10a
Brentano's (New York) A2b, 5, 6a, 9b, 10a, 11, 12a, 16
Brentano's Ltd. (London) A10b
British Broadcasting Corporation A5, 7
British Council, The B5
British Library A1a, 2a, 4, 6a, 7, 8a, 10b, 11, 12a, c, d, 13a, b, 19a, 21, 24, 27, Ap
'Broken Orchid, A' **C8**
Brooke, Jocelyn A28; B3, 5
Brophy, Brigid B10
Buckle, Richard A7
Buhrer, Albert A4; *see also* Bury, Adrian; Tell
Burn (James) and Company Ltd. (London) A3
Burleigh Press (Bristol) A10c
Bury, Adrian, *see* Buhrer, Albert
Butler, Samuel A9a

Caliban Press, The (New York) A8b
Camelot Press Ltd. (London) A10c
Campbell, Archie A7
Caprice A2a, 3, 5, 6a, 9a, 10a, 12a, c, d, 17a; Ms 11
Carewe, Helen A8a; Ms 11
Centaur Press (London) A12a, 13b, 14
'Centenarians of Glennyfury, The' *see* Valmouth
Century Play Co. (New York) A10a

101

INDEX

Chapman, Guy A12a
Charles V, Emperor A24
Cherry Lane Theatre (New York) A10a
Cleverdon, Douglas A5
Clodd, Alan A21; Ms 13
Cobden-Sanderson, Richard B4
Cochran, Charles B. A10a
Collected Works of Ronald Firbank, The, see Works of Ronald Firbank, The
Columbia Essays on Modern Writers B9
Columbia University, Rare Book and Manuscript Library of Ms 6a, b, 7a, 14, 15, 22, 24
Columbia University, Jack H. Samuels Library A4; Ms 21
Columbia University Press (New York) B9
Complete Ronald Firbank, The A17a-b, 18
Concerning the Eccentricities of Cardinal Pirelli A11, 12a, c, d, 12f, 13a, 15, 18, 19a; Ms 23; Ts 1.1
Congress, Library of A2b, 10a, 12b, e, f, 15, 19b, 22, 26
Connolly, Cyril A28
Conrad, Joseph A9a
Cornhill Magazine C9; Ts 6
Count Fanny's Nuptials (Arrow) Ap
Courier, The (Camden, New Jersey) A9b
Coward-McCann Inc. (New York) A10a, 12e, f, 15
Cox & Wyman Ltd. (London) A18
Crackanthorpe, Hubert A1a
Crane, Walter A28
Cunard, Nancy A10a, B4

Daedalus Press (Stoke Ferry) A24, 27
Daily Mirror (London) A19a
Davidson, John A9a
De La More Press, The (London) A13a, b
'Disciple from the Country, A' Ts 2
Donohue, Mrs A. McNeill Ms 6a, b, 14, 15, 22, 24
Double Dealer, The (New Orleans, Louisiana) A10a
Dowson, Ernest A21
'Drama in Sunlight' see *Prancing Nigger*; *Sorrow in Sunlight*
Duckworth (Gerald) & Co. Ltd. (London) A6b, c, 9a, 10c, 12a, c, d, 13a, b, 17a, b, 19a; B2, 11
Duke, Vernon A10a
Duncan, Harry A22
Duveen, Sir Joseph A7

Early Flemish Painter, An A24; C5.1
Easton, Hugh A13b
Elder Dempster Lines A10a
Elkin Mathews (London) A1a, b, 10a
Elliott and Fry (London) A19a
'Enchanted Princess, The' A15; see *The Artificial Princess*
England, Elizabeth A10a
English Authors Series B8
English Catalogue A10b
English Novelists, The B3
Enitharmon Press (London) A24, 27, 29
Evans, C. S. A10a
Evans, Edith A7
Evans, Montgomery A16
Eve A9a
Extravaganzas A15
Exzentrizitäten des Kardinals Pirelli Betreffend, Die A25; see *Concerning the Eccentricities of Cardinal Pirelli*

'Fairies Wood, The' Ap
Fales Collection, New York University Library MS 9, 12, 16; Ts 11, 13
'Fantasia for Orchestra in F Sharp Minor' C7
Far Away A22; Ms 1; Ts 2.1
Ferguson, William (Cambridge, Massachusetts) A26
Fielding, Fenella A6a
Firbank, Arthur Annesley Ronald, Photographs of A17a, b, 19a, b; B7a, b, 10; C10; portraits of A9a, b, 11, 12a, b, d, 17a, b, 18; B2, 7a, b, 10, 11 *et passim*
Firbank, Lady Harriette Jane Garrett A2a, 4, 8a, 9a, 10a, 19a: B6, 7a; Ap
Firbank, Heather A4, 10a, 19a; B6, 7a, 8b
Firbank, Joseph Sydney Ap
Firbank, Sir Joseph Thomas A1b
Firbank, Ronald, see Firbank, Arthur Annesley Ronald
Firbank, Lt.-Col. Thomas A10a, B4

INDEX

Firbank papers (FP) A19a; Ms 1, 2, 3, 4, 5, 6a, b, 7a, 8a, b, 9, 10, 12, 13, 14, 15, 16, 17, 18, 19, 21, 22, 23, 24; Ts 2, 3, 4, 5, 6, 7, 8a, 9, 10, 11, 12a, b, 13
Fish, A. H. A5
Five Novels A12d, e, f; p. 64
Fletcher, Ifan Kyrle A13a; B2, 11
Flower Beneath the Foot, The **A9a–b**, 11, 12a, c, d, f, 17a, 20; Ms 21
Folkard, (R.) and Son (London) A1a
Fuà, Laura Lovisetti A19.1, 23

Gallimard (Paris) A16
Garden City Press Ltd. (Letchworth) A4, 5, 17a
Garnier-Pagès, Mlle Dora A9a, b
Garnier-Pagès, Mme Mathieu A9a, b
Gauguin, Paul A6a, 10a
Gay (Noel) Music Co. (London) A6a
General Strike A11
George V A9a
Gershwin, George A10a
Giles, Althea A5
'Glenmouth: A Romantic Novel' *see Valmouth*
'Glennyfurry: A Romance' *see Valmouth*
Golden Cross Inn (Oxford) C7
Golding, Louis A13b
Goldring, Douglas A10a
Gorelik, Mordecai A10a
Gorey, Edward A26
Gossaert, Jan A24
Granta, The A26; C4, 5, 6, 11
Granta 75, C4, 5, 11
Grillige Levan van Kardinal Pirelli gevolgd door Valmouth, Het **A28**; see *Concerning the Eccentricities of Cardinal Pirelli*; *Valmouth*
Grove Press (New York) A8b
Guevara, Alvaro B2

Hammerton, Stephen A5
Hanser (Carl) Verlag (Munich) A25
Hare, Doris A6a
Harmonie A27; C2; Ms 2; *see also Princesse aux Soleils & Harmonie, La*
Harris, Alan A19a
Hart, Moss A10a
Hart-Davis (Rupert), Ltd. (London) B6
Heinemann (William) Ltd. (London) A10a

"Her Dearest Friend" Ts 3
Herold, C. J. A11
Hill of Dreams, The (Machen) A2a
Hobson, Anthony B4
Holland, Vyvyan B. B2
Hollins (Frank) (London) Ms 11
Horan, Thomas Ms 11
Horder, Lord Mervyn B11; Ms 2
Horrocks, Sidney A14
Houghton Library, Harvard University Ms 17
How to Detect Beardsley Forgeries (Walker) Ap
Humanities Research Center, University of Texas at Austin Ms 10, 18
Huxley, Aldous A2a
Huxley, Maria (Mrs Aldous) A2a

'Ideas & Fancies' A19a; Ms 2
'If Julia . . .' Ms 12
Ilundain y Esteban, Archbishop A4, 11
'Impression d'Automne' A19a; C3; Ts 4; *see also* 'Souvenir d'Automne'
Inclinations A2a, 3, 5, 9a, 12a, c, d, 23; Ms 16; Ts 5
Inclinazioni A23; *see also Inclinations*
Iowa, University of A22
Irving Theatre (London) A7
Isabella, Infanta A1b

'Jazz Fantasy, A' (Macauley and Rose) A10a
John, Augustus A5, 6, 9a, 11, 12a, d, 18; B2, 7a, b, 11
Johnston, Albert A10a
Johnstone, G. G. Hope Ap
Jones, Ernest A12d
Jullian, Philippe A6b, 27
Jurgen (Cabell) A10a

Kaulak (Madrid) A19a
Kennard, Sir Coleridge A12a, 13a, b, 15, 29; Ts 11
Kennard, Lady A13b
King and His Navy and Army, The (London) C3
Knopf, Alfred A. (New York) A10a; B7a
Knopf, Blanche W. (New York) A9a
Komrij, Gerrit A28

'Lady Appledore's Mésalliance' A19a; C9; Ts 6
Laine, Cleo A6a

INDEX

La Touche, John A10a
Laughlin, James A12e, f, 17b, 19b, 20
Lavendar of Bromley A19a
'Lay of the Last Nurserymaid' B7a; Ms 3
Legend of Saint Gabriel, The Ts 7
Lehmann, Hyazinth *see* Reeck, Emerick
"Les Essais". Revue Mensuelle (Paris) A27; C1, 2
Letter from Arthur Ronald Firbank to Madame Albani, A **A14**
'Letter from Ronald Firbank to Carl Van Vechten, A' A29
Lewis, Wyndham A9a, b, 12a; B2
"Lieutenant & the Irise's Wife, The" Ms 2
['Lila'] B7a; Ms 4
Locher, Robert E. A10a
Longmans, Green & Co. (London) B5
Lovelace, Geoffrey A2a
Lyric Theatre (Hammersmith) A6a

Macauley, Thurston A10a
McCarthy, Lillah A7
Machen, Arthur A2a
Macmillan (London) B10
Manchester Guardian A12d
Manchester Public Libraries Reference Library Subject Catalogue Section 094 Private Press Books **A14**
Mary, Princess A9a
Mary, Queen A9a
Matisse, Henry A23
"Mauve Tower, The" Ts 8a–b
Meredith, George A9a
Merritt, James Douglas B8
Metro-Goldwyn-Mayer (Hollywood) A10a
Meulenhoff Editie (Amsterdam) A28
Moeller, Philip A10a
Moore, T. Sturge A9a
Morgan, Hon. Evan A2a, 7, 9a
Morning Post (London), A10b
"Mr. White-Morgan The Diamond King" Ms 5a–b
Muir, P. H. A1b, 10b
Murray Printing Co., The (New York) A20
Murry, J. Middleton B4
Mushlin, M. H. Ts 9

Narratori Vallecchi A23
Nation, The (New York) A12e
National Book League (London) B5
Nevinson, C. R. W. A9a, b, 10b; B2
New Directions (New York) A6c, 12e, f, 17b, 19b, 20; p. 64
New Directions Paperbook Edition **A20**
New Readers Library Edition **A10c**; *see also Prancing Nigger*
New Rythum, The A19a; B4; **C10**; Ms 6a–c, 23, 24
New Rythum and Other Pieces, The **A19a–b**; B4; C3, 9, 10; Ms 4, 5a; Ts 4, 6, 8a, 11, 12a, 13
New Shakespeare Theatre (Liverpool) A6a
New Statesman (London) A10b
New York Herald Tribune Books A12b
New York Post A2b, 9b
New York Times, The A15
New York Times Book Review, The A2b, 12a
New Yorker, The A12e
Nicolson, Sir Harold A2a
Nicolson, Mrs Harold A9a; *see also* Sackville-West, Vita (Hon. Victoria)
Nicolson, Lady Mary A9a
Noble Essences (Sitwell) A12e; C7
Noorda, Bob A23
Notebooks Ms 14–24
Nouvelle Revue Française, La (Paris) A16

Odette A Fairy Tale for Weary People A4, 5, 8a, 9a, 10a, 12a, 17a; B2; Ts 9
Odette D'Antrevernes **A1b**
Odette D'Antrevernes and A Study in Temperament **A1a, b**
d'Offay, Anthony Ms 8b, 19, Ap
Officine Grafiche, Le (Florence) A23
Omnibus Edition A12d–e; p. 64
Oppertshäuser, Otto A25
Orcoma, R. M. S. A10a
Owen, Faith A7

Park, Bertram (London) A19a
Paul, Brenda Dean A7
Payen-Payne, de Vincheles B2
Peacock, Walter A10a

INDEX

Peacock and Goddard (London) A7
Peat (W. B.) and Company (London) A9a
Penguin Modern Classics Edition **A18**
Phototype Ltd. (London) A12d, e
Pilloried! (Stokes) **B1**
Portfolio No. 7 (New York) C10; Ms 6b
Potoker, Benjamin A29
Potoker, Bessie A29
Potoker, Edward Martin A29; B9
Powell, Anthony A17a
Pozzi, Jean Ts 8a
Prancing Nigger A9b, 10a-c, 12a, c, d, f, 16, 18, 20; C8; Ms 22; *see also Sorrow in Sunlight; Princesse Artificielle Suivi de Mon Piaffeur Noir, La*
Prancing Novelist A Defence of Fiction in the Form of a Critical Biography in Praise of Ronald Firbank (Brophy) B10
Preface, *The Flower Beneath the Foot* A9b; Ms 7a, b
Princess Zoubaroff, The A7, 9a, 10a, 12a, c; Ms 14, 18, 19
Princesse Artificielle Suivi de Mon Piaffeur Noir, La **A16**
Princesse aux Soleils Romance Parlée, La A27; **C1**; Ms 8a, b; *see also Princesse aux Soleils & Harmonie, La*
Princesse aux Soleils & Harmonie, La A27; C1, 2; *see also Princesse aux Soleils Romance Parlée, La* and *Harmonie*
Printemps, Yvonne A16
Publishers' Weekly (New York) A2b, 9b, 10a, 12b, e, 15
Putnam's Sons, G. P. (New York) A5, 7, 10a
Pye label A6a

Rainbow Edition A10c, 12c, d; B2
Reading, Bertice A6a
'Recent Genius, A' (Stokes) B1
Reeck, Emerick A16
Reverie and Flavia Ms 9
Reviewer, The (Richmond, Virginia) A10a; C8
Richards, Frances A29
Richards, Grant A2a, 3, 5, 6a, 7, 8a, 9a, 10a, 11, 19a; B1, 2, 6, 7a
Richards (Grant) Ltd. (London) A2a, 3, 4, 5, 6, 7, 8a, 9a, 11

Richards Press Ltd. Publishers, The (London) B1; *see also* Richards (Grant) Ltd. (London)
Rivers, Larry C10
Riverside Press Ltd. (Edinburgh) A2a, 3, 6a, 7, 8a, 11
Rizzoli Editore (Milan) A19.1
Roberts (John) Press Ltd. (London) A21
Rochester University Library Ts 10, 12a
Roditi, Eduard A15
Ronald Firbank (Brooke) **B3**
Ronald Firbank (Merritt) **B8**
Ronald Firbank (Potoker) **B9**
Ronald Firbank and John Betjeman (Brooke) **B5**
Ronald Firbank A Biography (Benkovitz) **B7a-b**; Ms 3, 4
Ronald Firbank, A Memoir (Fletcher) A13a; **B2**, 11
Ronald Firbank, Memoirs and Critiques (Horder) **B11**
Rops, Felicien A2a, b
Roscoe, Mrs A9a
Rose, Stuart A2b, 5, 9b, 10a, 16; B6, 7a; Ms 7b
'Roses were never Called . . . , The' Ms 10
Rothenstein, Albert *see* Rutherston, Albert
Rothenstein, William A11
Rutherston, Albert A3

Sachs, Maurice A16
Sackville-West, Vita (Hon. Victoria) A2a; *see also* Nicolson, Mrs Harold
'Salome, or 'Tis a Pity that She Would' Ts 1a; *see Artificial Princess, The*
Samuels, Jack H. A4; Ms 21
Samuels (Jack H.) Library, Columbia University A4; Ms 21
Santal **A8a-b**, 9a, 12a, 17; Ms 11, 20, 21
Saville Theatre (London) A6a
Secker, Martin A2a
Seltzer, Thomas (New York) A10a
Sentimental Studies (Crackanthorpe) A1a
Sevier, Michel A7
Seville, Cardinal Archbishop of *see* Ilundain y Esteban, Archbishop
Shannon, Charles A11, 12a, d

105

INDEX

Shelton, James A10a
Shepheard's Hotel (Cairo) A 19a
Singing Bird & The Moon, The Ts 10
Sitwell, Dame Edith A2a; B4
Sitwell, Sir Osbert A2a, 12d, f; B2; C7
Sitwell, Sacheverell A2a
Sitwells A8a
Skelton's Press (Wellingborough) A29
Smith, Claude Jr. Ts 5
Smith (W. H.) & Son (London) A2a
Société Générale d'Imprimerie et d'Édition (Paris) A16
Society of Authors A9a, 10b, 12a, c
Somerset, Ragland B7a
Sorrow in Sunlight A10a, b; *see also* Prancing Nigger
Sotheby & Co.'s Catalogue of Nineteenth-Century & Modern First Editions, Presentation Copies, Autograph Letters, & Important Literary Manuscripts . . . A19a; B4
'Souvenir d'Automne' A19a, C3; Ts 4; *see also* 'Impression d'Automne'
Stokes, Sewell B1
Strang, William A5
'Study in Opal, A' A26, C6; *see also* Two Early Stories
Study in Temperament, A A1a, 19a

Talboys, R. St. Clair A1a
Tatler, The (London) A9a
Tavistock Repertory Company, The A7
Tell *see* Buhrer, Albert
Testa, Valerie A7
Three Novels A12d, e
Time (New York) A12e
Times, The (London) A7, 10b
Times Literary Supplement A1a, 5, 12d, 13a
Totheroh, Dan A10a
Tower Theatre (Islington) A7
Town Topics (London) A5
'Tragedy in Green A' A29; Ts 11
Trinity Press, The (Worcester) A19a
"True Love" Ts 12a-b
Truscott (James) & Son, Ltd. (London) A12d
Twayne Publishers, Inc. (Boston) B8
Two Early Stories A26, C4, 5, 6, 11; *see also* 'Study in Opal, A' and 'Wavering Disciple, The'

Typographic Laboratory (University of Iowa) A22

University College London, Library of A2a
Unwin Bros. Ltd. (London) A10b

Vainglory A2a-b, 3, 5, 9a, 12a, c, d; Ms 15
Vallecchi Editore (Florence) A23
Valmouth A6a-c, 9a, 10a, 12a, c, d, f, 16, 18; C7; Ms 17, 18
Vanagloria A19.1; *see also Vainglory*
Van Boekhoven-Bosh bv (Utrecht) A28
Van Vechten, Carl A1b, 4, 7a, 9a, 10a, 11, 13a, 19a, 29; B2, 6; C6, 8; Ms 4
Vaughan, Keith A12d

Waley, Arthur A12a, 25
Walker, R. A. Ap
Walton, W. T. A2a
Warhol, Andrew A12e
Watergate Theatre (London) A7
Waugh, Evelyn A28; B4
'Wavering Disciple, The' A26; C4-5, 11
Weidenfeld and Nicolson (London) B7b
Wellington College A1a
Westminster Press, The (London) A12a
' "When Widows Love" ' A29, Ts 13
When Widows Love & A Tragedy in Green Two Stories A29; *see also* 'Tragedy in Green, A' and ' "When Widows Love" '
Whibley, Charles A9a
Wiggins, George A2a, 3, A9a
Willmer Brothers and Co. Ltd. (Birkenhead) A6b
Wilson, Edmund A28
Wilson, Sandy A6a
"*Wind & The Roses, The*" A21; Ms 13
Works of Ronald Firbank, The A6b, 10c, 12a-f, 13b, 17, 23; Ts 5
Writers and Their Work B5

'Yew Trees and Peacocks' (Crackanthorpe) A1a
York Playhouse (New York) A6a
Young Visiters (Ashford) Ms 4

Zuleika Dobson (Beerbohm) A2a